NEW YORK RANGERS

MILLENNIUM MEMORIES

DAILY NEWS

Sports Publishing Inc.
www.dailynewsbooks.com

DAILY ◉ NEWS

JEFFREY JAY ELLISH, Coordinating Editor
CLAUDIA MITROI AND VICTORIA J. MARINI, Developmental Editors

ERIC MESKAUSKAS AND ANGELA TROISI, Photo Editors
SUSAN M. MCKINNEY, Director of Production
SCOT MUNCASTER, Book Layout
ERIN SANDS, Book Layout
TERRY NEUTZ HAYDEN, Interior Design
TODD LAUER, Dustjacket Design
JOHN HALLIGAN, Research Assistance
DAVID HAMBURG, Copy Editor

THE NEW YORK DAILY NEWS, Front & Back Cover Photos

ISBN 1-58261-134-3

Sports Publishing Inc.
www.dailynewsbooks.com

Printed in the United States

Acknowledgments

When talk turns to the subject of hockey's greatest franchises, the Original Six teams are at the epicenter of the discussion. The Chicago Blackhawks, Montreal Canadiens, Toronto Maple Leafs, Boston Bruins, Detroit Red Wings and New York Rangers kept hockey on the international stage with superb entertainment and endearing figures. Emerging from this historical group is the Rangers. From the beginning, the Rangers have been a franchise that has stood for class, innovation, and success.

The *Daily News* has given its readers a front-row seat for every historic moment of this great franchise. When the Rangers clinched their first Stanley Cup in 1928, the *Daily News* was there with pictures and stories of every dramatic twist. Even now, as the Rangers are the focus of such national stories as the team's magical run to the Cup in 1994 and the 1999 retirement of No. 99, the game's greatest player, the *Daily News* has continued to provide Ranger fans with the most complete and cogent coverage of the NHL's premier team.

Bringing the memories of Ranger hockey to life every day in the pages of the *Daily News* requires the hard work and dedication of hundreds of people at the paper. When we first approached the *Daily News* about this project, we received the overwhelming support of Ed Fay (VP/Director of Editorial Administration) and Les Goodstein (Executive Vice President/Associate Publisher). Among others at the paper who were instrumental in assisting us in this project were Lenore Schlossberg, John Polizano, Eric Meskauskas, Mike Lipak, Angela Troisi, Vincent Panzarino, Faigi Rosenthal, Peter Edelman, and Scott Browne. From the *Daily News* sports department, we specifically want to acknowledge the support of editor Leon Carter.

Space limitations preclude us from thanking all the writers and photographers whose contributions appear in this book. However, wherever available, we have preserved the writers' bylines and the photographers' credits to ensure proper attribution for their work.

And finally, I am grateful for all the support and hard work of those at Sports Publishing Inc. who worked tirelessly on this project: Joe Bannon, Jr., Erin Sands, Susan McKinney, Terry Hayden, Scot Muncaster, Victoria Marini, Claudia Mitroi, Julie Denzer, Todd Lauer, David Hamburg, and Crystal Gummere.

Jeffrey Jay Ellish
Coordinating Editor

Table of Contents

MEMBERS OF THE RANGERS' 1928 STANLEY CUP CHAMPIONSHIP TEAM.

1994 STANLEY CUP CELEBRATION.

RANGERS-MAROONS ON ICE TONIGHT

NOVEMBER 16, 1926

King Ice will rule supreme tonight at the new Madison Square Garden when the New York Rangers meet the world champion Montreal Maroons in the Rangers' first-ever hockey game. The proceeds of this game are for the benefit of the Grosvenor Neighborhood House.

The Garden has been transformed into a veritable winter palace, and a pretentious program has been arranged between periods for the entertainment of hockey patrons, including Katie Schmidt's ice ballet; West Point's cadet orchestra of 126 pieces also has been secured.

Neither the Rangers nor the Maroons were able to indulge in a regular practice game because of the short time available to put the Garden in readiness. Manager Lester Patrick, however, declared that it wasn't necessary for his team to have any further practice.

In the lineup for the Rangers will be Hal Winkler, goaltender; Taffy Abel of Saulte Ste. Marie and the only American-born player on the team, playing right defense; Ching Johnson of Winnipeg, left defense; Frank Boucher of Ottawa and formerly of the Vancouver Maroons of the Pacific League, center; Bill Cook of Kingston, Ontario, right wing; and Bun Cook, brother of Bill Cook, left wing.

OPPOSITE: NEW YORK'S FIRST PROFESSIONAL HOCKEY TEAM, THE AMERICANS, DREW SO WELL AT THE NEW MADISON SQUARE GARDEN IN 1925-26 THAT GARDEN PRESIDENT GEORGE "TEX" RICKARD PURCHASED HIS OWN NHL FRANCHISE FOR THE 1926-27 SEASON. DUBBED "TEX'S RANGERS," THE TEAM HAS KEPT ITS NICKNAME FOR NEARLY 75 YEARS. IN THEIR DEBUT AGAINST MONTREAL, THE RANGERS WON 1-0.

LESTER PATRICK
BECOMES GOALIE

APRIL 8, 1928

Frank Boucher's goal after seven minutes of overtime play gave the New York Rangers a 2-to-1 victory over the Montreal Maroons in the second game of the Stanley Cup finals for the championship of the National Hockey League tonight. The standing is now one match all.

The Maroons finally got a break when Munro and Stewart got around each side of the Ranger defense on a fast combination play. Stewart took Munro's pass, and his fast backhand shot caught Lorne Chabot in the left eye. The Ranger goalie fell to the ice and had to be assisted from the rink in great pain. The referee ordered both teams to their dressing rooms while the visiting netminder was being attended to.

After twenty minutes' delay, it was announced that Lester Patrick, veteran Ranger manager, would don the pads and replace the injured Chabot, who meantime had been rushed to a hospital with an eye hemorrhage.

In a conference with league and team officials, the Rangers asked if they might use Alex Connell, Ottawa goalie, who was in the building. The Maroons balked, however, at allowing their opponents the use of one who is considered in many quarters the league's best goalie, and it was decided that the Rangers must use one of their own men.

On the resumption of play, the Rangers started playing a strong back-checking game in order to give Patrick as much protection as possible. Bill Cook got in for the first shot on goal, but Benedict handled his effort handily. Play had been in progress fully five minutes before Patrick had his first shot to handle. It was a weak play into New York territory.

The Maroons tied the score at 14:20 when Stewart scored on Hooley Smith's rebound. There was no further scoring in this period and the game went into overtime.

OPPOSITE: EN ROUTE TO A STANLEY CUP VICTORY IN 1928, RANGERS MANAGER LESTER PATRICK DONNED GOALIE PADS IN AN EMERGENCY STINT AS GOALKEEPER, REPLACING AN INJURED LORNE CHABOT.

RANGERS WIN STANLEY CUP MILLER, BOUCHER STAR

APRIL 15, 1928

The Stanley Cup went tonight to the United States for the second time, when the New York Rangers scored a 2-to-1 victory over the Montreal Maroons in the fifth and deciding game of the 1928 hockey world series.

The game was the best of the current series and was witnessed by one of the largest crowds of the season, 12,000 fans jamming their way into the forum. It was a great game for the Gothamites to win.

The locals held a wide margin in territorial play throughout and outshot the opposition practically two to one. The stumbling block in their way, however, was Joe Miller, whose display in the Rangers' net stamped him as the hero of the series.

Miller, who was brought in as a substitute when Chabot, regular New York netminder, was hurt in the second game, stamped himself as one of the world's leading goalkeepers. His work tonight was the more impressive by the fact that he received a stick between the eyes in the first period and had to play the rest of the game with a badly swollen face. It was a game of heroic display.

However, Miller was not the only hero on the ice. Frank Boucher, Ranger center, scored both New York goals on brilliant individual efforts. Both counters were scored in a similar manner. On the two occasions, Boucher broke following sustained Montreal attacks and took the Maroon defense unawares. On the first one, he stepped between Siebert and Dutton and had little trouble in beating Benedict. This was late in the first period. In the third period, with all Maroons on the attack but Munro and Benedict, Boucher suddenly broke away again, outguessed Munro and then beat the unprotected Maroon goalie.

FRANK BOUCHER, VETERAN CENTER OF THE NEW YORK RANGERS, HELPED THE RANGERS WIN THE STANLEY CUP IN 1928 AND 1933.

BOSTONS NIP RANGERS, 2-1, FOR STANLEY CUP

BY PAT ROBINSON   MARCH 30, 1929

The Rangers had staged a great uphill fight to tie the score in the final session after the Bruins had taken a one-goal lead in the second spasm. Then, with only two minutes left to play, Harry Oliver and Bill Carson teamed up in a neat little sketch that sent the title up to the Hub.

The game was rough and fast throughout, with honors about even all the way until that one fatal move just before the bell.

Harry Oliver, a hard-shooting wingman, put Boston out in front late in the second chapter. He took a pass from Eddie Shore at his own line, skidded past the Ranger forwards and stickhandled his way between Taffy Abel and Sparky Vail. Once past them, it was a simple matter to lure Roach to one side and grab his goal.

You could have cut the gloom in the Garden with a knife until the Rangers, battling as only a fading champ can, staged their comeback early in the third session.

Bill Cook and Frank Boucher carried the puck into the tight Bruin defense in a series of desperate rushes. Time after time they missed goals by the skin of their teeth. Then came a face-off near the net, and Murray Murdoch, who was the best man on the ice all night, slapped the puck back to Butch Keeling.

Butch grabbed it near the blue line and flung a high-sailing shot that cleared Tiny Thompson's waist and put the Rangers on even footing. For the moment, their crown, which had been badly tilted over one ear, straightened up. But only for such time as it took the Bruins to find the correct combination for a score.

They won because they were strongest where we were weakest.

The Bruins richly deserved their honors, and we wish them a long reign and all that sort of rot, but damn it, I wish Gaby Des Lys hadn't set that fashion.

OPPOSITE: FROM ONE IRON MAN TO ANOTHER. LOU GEHRIG, WHO'S PLAYED IN 1,307 CONSECUTIVE GAMES WITH THE YANKS, PRESENTS A RING TO MURRAY MURDOCH, WHO HAS TAKEN PART IN EVERY ONE OF THE RANGERS' 400 GAMES. JOHN REED KILPATRICK (CENTER), PRESIDENT OF GARDEN CORPORATION, AND BILL COOK LOOK ON.

IT'S ALL OVER!
LEAFS WIN, 6-4!

APRIL 10, 1932

The youthful, speeding Maple Leafs of Toronto tonight brought the Stanley Cup to this Ontario metropolis by defeating the New York Rangers, 6-4, in the third of their three-out-of-five-game series for the time-worn trophy and the world's professional hockey championship.

The victory gave the Leafs the series in three straight games, the first time the cup has ever been won in that fashion. Coupled with their 6-to-4 win in New York and 6-to-2 triumph in Boston, the Leafs earned the praise of the fans by their brilliant victory tonight.

Each team scored once in the second period.

Frank Boucher, Ranger center, broke through for New York's first goal. The play was started by Ott Heller. From his own defense, Heller skated down the ice to give Frank the disk, and the hard shot sifted into the net between Chabot's pads.

The third period saw six goals scored. Frank Finnigan took Day's pass to make it 4-1 for the Leafs, and Bailey combined with Conacher and Day to add another. The desperate Rangers then swept in, with Bill Cook taking Boucher's pass for a goal. Bob Gracie kept up the new scoring line's reputation for the Leafs by counting on Finnigan's pass.

Frank Boucher culminated a great night's work by scoring twice within two minutes near the end of the game. He took Bun Cook's pass in front of the net to make the first goal and then went through on a beautiful solo rush for the second.

The attendance created a near-record, the unofficial estimate placing the crowd at 14,500.

New York Rangers' Fred "Bun" Cook was a powerful scorer who was in the top 10 three times in nine seasons. Playing for the Rangers from 1926 to 1936, Cook helped his team get to the Stanley Cup Finals four times. Cook was inducted into the Hockey Hall of Fame in 1995.

BILL COOK'S GOAL GIVES RANGERS STANLEY CUP

APRIL 14, 1933

The New York Rangers reascended hockey's heights tonight, defeating the Toronto Maple Leafs, 1-0, in overtime, to clinch the Stanley Cup and the world's professional championship.

Two Ranger veterans, Bill Cook and Butch Keeling, combined to break up the fourth and, as it turned out, the decisive struggle of the cup series after 7 minutes and 33 seconds of overtime play.

For the Rangers, it was their second Stanley Cup victory in five years. The Rangers of the 1927-28 season won the coveted trophy by beating the Montreal Maroons.

Through the first sixty minutes of regulation play, the Leafs held a wide edge on the attack, but they could not beat Andy Aitkenhead, young Ranger goalie.

Aitkenhead stopped 48 drives during the first three periods.

Then came the "break." Levinsky sent Ossie Asmundson, Ranger forward, sprawling with a too-heavy body check and was banished. Joe Primeau and Murdoch got tangled up in another face-off, and suddenly Keeling spurted up to the scramble, poked the puck clear and started away. The crowd of 13,500 rose almost as one man as Keeling raced over the Toronto blue line, pulled Clancy over his way and tossed a pass on Cook's stick. One of the greatest marksmen in hockey history, Cook promptly fired it into a corner of the net to score the winning "sudden-death" goal.

The Rangers set a new record by coming up from third place to win the cup.

OPPOSITE: BILL COOK WON THE LEAGUE SCORING TITLE IN 1933 WHILE LEADING THE RANGERS TO THEIR SECOND STANLEY CUP CHAMPIONSHIP IN FIVE YEARS.

CHING AND UNCLE SAM TEAM IN PAY WAR

BY JIMMY POWERS   OCTOBER 30, 1934

Uncle Sam may not realize it now, but he is going to be a powerful intermediary in all future baseball and hockey holdout wars. The dictatorial role of the old gentleman in the red-and-white striped trousers and close-cropped goatee was revealed yesterday when the sagacious Ching Johnson, daring old man on the flying steel skates, unbosomed himself in the offices of Madison Square Garden. Ching is the sole Ranger holdout.

"After January 1 all incomes for the year 1934 will be open to public inspection at the U.S. Internal revenue office," explained the Rangers' star defenseman and New York's leading gallery god. "This will give holdouts a strong weapon. I wish I had that information now. I wouldn't be cooling my heels here."

Johnson, a big draw at the box office, is asking for $7,000, the league limit, although his pull in trade is probably worth much more. But he has to take Colonel John S. Hammond's word that other stars on the Rangers are paid less than $7,000, that operating expenses are high, that the club cannot afford to pay him more, and that admissions last season totaled only $270,000.

Under the new law, Dizzy Dean or Johnson, or anyone, for that matter, must file a special slip containing gross income, deductions, net income, total credits and the amount of tax payable.

Ching Johnson, anxious to discover if the good Colonel Hammond was apple-saucing him with his cries of poverty, attempted yesterday to inspect income tax returns filed in March of this year under the belief that the law was proactive.

OPPOSITE: A FOUR-TIME NHL ALL-STAR AND HALL OF FAME MEMBER, THE RANGERS' IVAN "CHING" JOHNSON WAS A HARD-NOSED DEFENSEMAN KNOWN FOR LEADING THE RANGERS IN PENALTY MINUTES IN EIGHT OF HIS 11 SEASONS WITH NEW YORK.

DILLON SPARK PLUG OF RANGER TEAM

FEBRUARY 13, 1938

The Rangers have 14 games to go till the playoffs—the crucial point of the season coming up. Here is a keen, finely balanced combination, but there is one man whom the other players look up to; one man who can be depended upon to deliver in the pinches—Cecil Dillon.

One of the cleverest sharpshooters in hockey today, Dillon's keen eye and hard shot have paced the Rangers to the threshold of the Stanley Cup playoffs. He's not an individualist but a real playmaker—and there lies his value to the Ranger organization.

He played his first junior hockey at Meaford, near his home in Thornbury, and then, at 18, he went to play for Owen Sound. One day he scored seven goals; one of those red-letter days as, at 29, he looks back on boyhood.

Then came the meeting with Lester Patrick—the man who was to influence the rest of his hockey career.

Dillon was sent to Springfield—then a Ranger farm club. After two years with Springfield, he had failed to show any big-time stuff. He pleaded to stay with the team, but Patrick saw some spark of greatness and brought him up to the Rangers.

And now Lester Patrick's estimate of Cecil is paying big dividends.

OPPOSITE: CECIL DILLON JOINED LYNN PATRICK AND MURRAY MURDOCH ON A LINE THAT REPLACED THE FAMOUS BOUCHER-COOK LINE IN 1935-36. PERHAPS BEST KNOWN FOR HIS DURABILITY (HE NEVER MISSED A REGULAR-SEASON GAME FOR THE RANGERS), DILLON WENT ON TO LEAD THE TEAM IN SCORING FOR THREE CONSECUTIVE YEARS, FROM 1935 TO 1938.

Rangers Win, Take Cup

By Gene Ward   April 14, 1940

Outclassed, 2-0, in the opening two periods here tonight, the Rangers turned in a tremendous comeback to tie up their sixth Stanley Cup tilt with the Maple Leafs, 2-2, and send it into sudden-death overtime. Syl Apps had counted for Toronto in the first session, Nick Metz in the second and 14,894 were all excited over a series-tying triumph from their heroes when the Rangers started to ride the icy plains. Socko!—Neil Colville shook Red Horner out of his hair and made it 2-1. One minute 54 seconds later in the third period, Alf Pike feinted goalie Broda out of position and delivered the tying goal.

The Rangers began to fly at Broda in the opening minutes as Phil Watson, Bryan Hextall and Dutch Hiller generated a flashy attack.

In the second period, Stanowski led a rush which wound up with Marker slamming a hard one which Kerr saved amid a tangle of arms and legs.

Syl Apps broke up the attack after Coulter, Watson and Muzz Patrick had openings. Apps sped away, passed to Dillon, but the latter wasted the shot on the backboards. Hiller was in there, but Broda was too quick for him, blocking a vicious

drive with a lunge. Horner was bounced for holding Hextall on the same rush and the Rangers went to work.

As 10 minutes approached, the Leafs began to grow more and more cautious, but at 8:08 Neil Colville took Shibicky's pass, untangled himself from Horner and banged a pretty angled shot into the net.

A moment later, Mac Colville and Schriner were ousted for slashing, and the Rangers cashed in for the tying goal. Alf Pike got it after taking Clint Smith's pass-out from the corner. Pike took the disk slightly to the right of Broda, took a quick step out in front of the cage, feinted once and let go high into the corner. The time was 10:02.

At 17:14 Watson, Hextall, Hiller, Coulter and Muzz Patrick ganged up on Broda. Watson was wide open for a shot and Hex had the disk, but Broda saved and there was a big pile-up with Broda on the bottom. The red light flashed, but Stewart ruled it no goal, although the Rangers protested long and loudly.

The Rangers won the game and the Stanley Cup on a goal by Hextall in 2:07 of the first overtime on passes from Watson and Hiller.

FOR SIX STRAIGHT SEASONS (1938-1944), THE RANGERS' BRYAN HEXTALL SCORED 20 GOALS—AN NHL RECORD AT THE TIME. BUT IT WAS HIS OVERTIME GOAL AGAINST TORONTO TO CLINCH THE RANGERS' 1940 STANLEY CUP CHAMPIONSHIP THAT ETCHED HIM FOREVER IN THE RANGER HISTORY BOOKS. LITTLE DID ANYONE KNOW THAT IT WOULD BE ANOTHER 54 YEARS BEFORE THE RANGERS WOULD AGAIN TASTE VICTORY FROM LORD STANLEY'S CUP. HEXTALL WAS SELECTED TO THE HOCKEY HALL OF FAME IN 1969.

Cook-to-Boucher-to-Cook Reunited for War Cause

Dick Young   January 27, 1944

Bill Cook, Frankie Boucher and Bun Cook are too old to enlist, but still young enough and capable enough to fire rubber slugs for the war effort. And so, this fabulous forward wall, greatest in hockey history, is being re-formed for a one-game stand in Sunday's glittering Fourth War Loan all-star tussle at the Garden.

The terrific trio of ex-Rangers is as eager to play together again local hockey fans are to catch an auld lang syne glimpse of them. Boucher beamed at the thought of being reunited with his old buddies, adding, "Get in touch with the Cleveland team (where Bill is general manager and Bun is coach). I'm positive they'll be as happy as I am to play together again."

As the famous line skates onto the Garden rink, veteran memories will drift back to 1926, when the newly organized Rangers set up their NHL franchise. They'll recall the precision passing, deft poke checking, and sizzling shooting which soon made the "Cook-to-Boucher-to-Cook" catch line a famous one.

For 10 years, the royal triumvirate upheld the Rangers as an NHL power. Eventually, Bill went to Cleveland as manager, Bun was sold to Providence, where he became coach, and Boucher was made pilot of the Rovers. Now, after a nine-year separation, they join other Gotham puck-pushing favorites in presenting the greatest hockey show ever offered fans—and for free to bond buyers!

OPPOSITE: BROTHERS BILL COOK (LEFT) AND BUN COOK (RIGHT) JOINED FRANKIE BOUCHER (CENTER) IN THE 1926-27 SEASON TO BECOME ONE OF THE TOP LINES IN NHL HISTORY. ALMOST 20 YEARS LATER, THEY TEAMED UP AGAIN FOR AN ALL-STAR EXHIBITION TO BENEFIT THE COUNTRY'S WAR EFFORT.

HELLER, HEXTALL CALLED IN DRAFT

BY HY TURKIN   FEBRUARY 1, 1944

Unlucky everywhere but in the box office—where they're currently cracking all records despite their chronic cellar standing—the Rangers are headed for another bizarre blow. Their offensive and defensive mainstays, Bryan Hextall and Capt. Ott Heller, are facing induction into the U.S. armed forces despite the fact that both are Canadian resident citizens.

The whole thing is a clerical oversight, and may be cleared up when the veteran Blueshirts pow-wow with Local Board No. 22 tonight. Under the advice of Madison Square Garden attorneys, the entire Ranger team registered during this country's first enrollment, in October '40. Local Selective Service headquarters yesterday said that the players were eligible within three months after that for a Certificate of Non-Residence, canceling registration liability, but they failed to apply; however, they still may be relieved of responsibility at the discretion of the board. Heller and Hextall, of course, are both registered with the Canadian draft boards. Under his country's rules, Heller, married and over 30, is not subject to call. But if he's called up locally, he still has the prerogative of joining the Army of his own country instead . . . which Heller says he would do. It's doubtful whether Ott, 33, could pass the Army physical, because he's had both shoulders broken and now is playing with an injured elbow that will be operated on as soon as the season is over.

With less than seven weeks remaining for the hockey season, manager Les Patrick has his fingers crossed for Hextall and Heller. Neither of his boys has been called for actual induction yet, and so he'll have them for at least a month. If the local "misunderstanding" can be ironed out, there's little doubt that the continued presence of the "H" boys will boost the Rangers to new eaon records. The local B.O. already has raked in more than $400,000.

OPPOSITE: DUE TO A CLERICAL GLITCH, RANGER DEFENSEMAN OTT HELLER (SHOWN TRAINING WITH HEAVY BAG) AND TEAMMATE BRYAN HEXTALL WERE FACING INDUCTION INTO THE U.S. MILITARY IN 1944, DESPITE THE FACT THAT BOTH HELLER AND HEXTALL WERE CANADIAN CITIZENS.

FRANK BOUCHER: HOCKEY VISIONARY

BY GENE WARD   OCTOBER 12, 1947

Rub your eyes and look again if you don't believe it, but the hockey season is off and running this week, with New York's revitalized Rangers playing their opener against Les Canadiens in Montreal next Thursday. All of which brings us to the man currently considered the most vital and astounding character in the game and one who, ordinarily, would need no introduction but for the fact that his activities are conducted with such machine-gun rapidity and in so many directions at once, that constant inventory is needed. We speak, naturally, of Francois Boucher.

Along with the Cook brothers, Boucher set all kinds of fancy records on the rink and made an unprecedented return to action at the age of 42, playing 15 games and clicking for four goals, 10 assists, as he stepped into the lineup to help out his war-ravaged Rangers.

After accepting a front-office position with the Rangers, Boucher pushed for league-wide reform. Advocating a more simplified language for NHL official rules, he rewrote the book. At the league's spring meeting in 1945, he was elected Chairman of the Rules Committee, and the fans, who love streamlined hockey, have been getting a break ever since. For a long time he had held big ideas on opening up the game, and when streamlined hockey finally arrived, it would have died a-borning, so to speak, if Frank hadn't sponsored the rules change which put in the red line and widened the passing territory. His next move was to bring the blue lines closer together, and his ultimate goal is a single line at center ice, thus putting the full accent on speed and offense.

OPPOSITE: DURING HIS CAREER IN THE NHL, FRANK BOUCHER WON THE LADY BYNG TROPHY SEVEN TIMES IN EIGHT YEARS BETWEEN 1927-35, EARNING HIM PERMANENT POSSESSION OF THE ORIGINAL TROPHY. AS A GENERAL MANAGER IN 1943-44, BOUCHER MADE A SMALL COMEBACK AND PLAYED IN 15 GAMES FOR THE RANGERS TO HELP OUT DURING THE PLAYER DEFICIT CAUSED BY THE WAR.

THE POWERHOUSE: BUDDY O'CONNOR

BY JIMMY POWERS   NOVEMBER 2, 1947

No other sport has been hit as hard by the recent war as hockey. A lot of ball players, gridiron stars and racqueteers managed to stay in shape on various camp, pre-flight and training teams. Some even improved. But not hockey players, for their sport demands specific playing and climatic conditions. By the same token, hockey players only grow in the ice latitudes. So the big trouble now is a shortage of talent, with the Canadian clubs, naturally, having the inside track. And look at your top scorers—the old men of the game. Syl Apps, 32; Maurice Richard, 26; Toe Blake, 35; Milt Schmidt, 29; Buddy O'Connor, 31; Elmer Lach, 29. Those are years, not goals. But the Rangers are making every attempt to lure top stars this way, and in this Buddy O'Connor, our man, M. Boucher, really came up with a corking good center. He is a left-handed shot, 5'-7", weighs 145, but gets down to 142 in mid-season, which makes him the lightest forward in the majors.

O'Connor was one of Montreal's best-liked athletes, and it is obvious he may well achieve the same status in New York. You cannot help liking the guy. There is nothing of the "I am" about him. When things go wrong with the club, there is never a word of criticism for anyone. When the breaks are coming, and generally it is Buddy who is making them, he is obviously uncomfortable when the bouquets are thrown his way.

Frank Boucher is tickled to have Buddy on his bench. In a sense, he is of the Boucher pattern. Quiet, retiring off the ice, a gentleman on the ice (no-penalties Boucher, you remember) and an accomplished artist in action by virtue of brains, deft stick-handling and clever maneuvers. Further, Buddy can, and Frankie could, score plenty of goals, too.

Well, Buddy is well on his way in the league scoring race. Let us hope this little shower of rose petals does not trip him up.

OPPOSITE: IN HERBERT WILLIAM "BUDDY" O'CONNOR'S FIRST SEASON WITH THE RANGERS (1947-48), HE HAD A BANNER YEAR WITH 24 GOALS AND 36 ASSISTS FOR 60 POINTS IN 60 GAMES. HE ALSO WON THE HART AND LADY BYNG TROPHIES THAT YEAR.

BLUES GET BOUNCED ON PATRICK NIGHT

BY DICK YOUNG   DECEMBER 4, 1947

As old and spavined as they might be, the Cooks, the Ching Johnsons, the Butch Keelings and the other old-timers who flocked to the Garden for Lester Patrick Night could have been used by the Rangers last evening. The new Ranger youngsters did their best to honor the old Blueshirt boss and his 43 years in hockey, but Toronto's tough Maple Leafs wound up using them for a springboard into first place in the NHL as they hammered the home boys, 4-1, before 15,925, a sellout crowd.

In fact, so inept was the current crop of locals during most of the penalty-packed battle that Bill and Bun Cook were seen being forcibly detained from climbing over the sideboards and entering the fray.

Among the many who came from far and wide to pay tribute to Lester Patrick on his "night" in the Garden last evening were most of the great Ranger players he developed during his years as mastermind of the New York six. There were those Ranger originals on hand for the pre-game ceremonies in which Lester was tabbed for hockey's Hall of Fame: Leo Bourgault, Paul Thompson, Murray Murdoch, Taffy Abel, Butch Keeling, Ott Heller and Lester's two sons, Lynn and Muzz. That great line, the Cook brothers, Bill and Bun, and Frank Boucher, even put on Ranger uniforms and skated out for the occasion. But the biggest hand of all went to Ching Johnson, the bald defenseman.

OPPOSITE: LESTER PATRICK, VETERAN MANAGER AND COACH OF THE NEW YORK RANGERS, GIVES HIS SON, LYNN PATRICK, SOME POINTERS. THE ELDER PATRICK SERVED AS COACH FOR THE INAUGURAL SEVEN YEARS OF THE RANGERS AND GM FOR THE FIRST 20.

Lund of Rangers Wins Calder Cup

May 3, 1949

Pentti Lund, 23-year-old Finnish-born right wing of the Rangers, today was named winner of the Calder Memorial Trophy as the NHL's outstanding rookie for the '48-'49 season.

Lund received six first-place votes, five seconds and three thirds for a total of 31 points in a poll of 18 NHL writers and radio broadcasters—three from each league city. In addition to the cup, Lund won a cash prize of $1,000.

Second to Lund among the 12 rookies who received consideration in the balloting was his teammate, defenseman Allan Stanley, who had five first-place votes and two seconds for 19 points. Ray Timgren, Maple Leaf right wing, was third with three firsts, one second and five thirds for a total of 16 points. The ballot was constructed on a 3-2-1 point basis.

The six-foot, 190-pound Lund scored 14 goals and 16 assists for 30 points, the highest total registered by a rookie during the season. Lund, born in Helsinki, is the second successive foreign-born player to win the Calder Trophy.

Opposite: Coach Lynn Patrick (second from right), who used to wear the No. 9 jersey, measures Pentti Lund for No. 9 as Duncan Fisher, Ed Slowinski and Tony Leswick look on. Lund was placed on "The Three-L Line" with Edgar Laprade and Leswick, and he won the Calder Cup as the NHL's outstanding rookie in the 1948-49 season.

CHUCK MAKES RAYNGERS GO

BY JIMMY POWERS   JANUARY 29, 1950

Chuck Rayner, who has been filling the nets for the Blue Shirts since he returned from the war, should be tabbed the All-Star goaltender of the National Hockey League. From the beginning of the Rangers' climb out of the loop cellar on Dec. 4 through New Year's Eve, Chuck allowed only 15 goals in 12 games. Three of those were "freaks."

Connie Smythe, Mr. Hockey up in Toronto, has been quoted as saying, "Rayner is the best goalie in the game today."

Don't think Chuck's job is a soft touch. For one thing, he generally handles more shots than the goalkeepers in the opposing nets. On many occasions the "Scoreless Scoundrels," as Gene Ward has labeled the Rangers, have failed to press much more than 20 or 22 shots on the opposition goaltender in the run of a game. Chuck, on the other hand, generally finds it necessary to repel 35 and 40 per contest.

Last season, on one weekend, he had 81 shots drilled at him. Of these, only one got by.

Chuck admits there were many times when failure on a given night had him on the verge of quitting the game.

He has realized since, of course, how important it is to brace himself after a nightmarish evening. Typical of Rayner, though, is the thought that he has four youngsters coming up. Aware that kids today are going through the same experiences, he often takes time to talk to youngsters.

In fact, his advice for an aspiring goalie is:

"Don't get panicky when you're badly beaten. Even when you're six goals behind, finish out the game as though it were a scoreless tie."

There are some opposing players who call our local sextet the *"New York Rayngers."* And why not? He's to the Blue Shirts what DiMag is to the Yanks.

CLARENCE S. CAMPBELL (LEFT), PRESIDENT OF THE NATIONAL HOCKEY LEAGUE, PRESENTS THE HART TROPHY TO CHUCK RAYNER (CENTER) AND THE LADY BYNG TROPHY TO EDGAR LAPRADE. IN THE 1949-50 SEASON, RAYNER HAD A 2.62 AVERAGE ALONG WITH SIX SHUTOUTS, HELPING HIS TEAM TO THE STANLEY CUP FINALS THAT YEAR.

LEGENDARY COOK BELONGS IN HALL

BY DANA MOZLEY   FEBRUARY 19, 1951

Although its permanent shrine is still to be built, hockey's Hall of Fame is already a sizable body. However, for one reason or another—prejudice or politics or just plain oversight, perhaps—it is not yet a representative body. It won't be until the best right winger in the game's history is a member.

There is no excuse for Bill Cook's absence from a list that now numbers 26 former players and 10 of the game's builders and executives. As dual member of the Hall of Fame Selection Committee and Governing Board, Art Ross of the Bruins sponsored both Eddie Shore and Dit Clapper for the award. Shore deserved it and Clapper may have . . . but only after Cook had been picked.

If you discount Lester Patrick, who was elected to the Hall for his playing record in Canada, the list is barren of Rangers.

Patrick apparently failed to plug for any of his old team when he was both a member of the organization and of the Hall of Fame Governing Board. The oversight should be corrected now, when the governors are preparing to vote in additional members.

Frank Boucher, a very eligible candidate himself since he was second only to Howie Morenz as a center, thinks it's about time the committee recognized the elder of the Cooks.

"Nine out of 10 people in Canada will tell you Bill was the greatest right wing of all time," the Blues' boss said yesterday. "He was an All-Star six straight seasons and, at the age of 36, when most players are long gone, he was not only an All-Star but led the league in scoring. He didn't arrive in the league until he was 30, and look at the record."

OPPOSITE: BILL COOK LED THE NHL IN GOALS THREE TIMES WHILE WINNING TWO SCORING TITLES IN NEW YORK. "NINE OUT OF 10 PEOPLE IN CANADA WILL TELL YOU BILL WAS THE GREATEST RIGHT WING OF ALL TIME," THEN-RANGERS COACH FRANK BOUCHER SAID IN 1951. COOK WOULD EVENTUALLY BE INDUCTED INTO THE HALL OF FAME IN AUGUST OF 1952.

PRENTICE JOINS RANGERS IN TIME FOR BRUIN TILT

BY HY TURKIN   DECEMBER 10, 1952

It's hard to believe any big-league hockey team would pay $7,500 for a Ranger castoff, but that's what happened when the last-place locals yesterday decided not to withdraw veteran left winger Gaye Stewart from the waiver list after the Canadiens had claimed him the night before.

No tears have been shed over Gaye's good-bye, because Dean Prentice, the 20-year-old rookie who beat him out of a regular job, leaves the injured list in time to face the Bruins here tonight.

Prentice missed last Sunday's game because of a wrenched knee, but he had scored three goals in his last six games, so the punch-seeking Rangers will welcome him back tonight. He's more aggressive than the 29-year-old Stewart and can skate faster—an important asset with the Rangers, who so often allow the enemy to fast-break against them.

Come game time tonight, the Rangers could use three like Prentice. Despite the fact that they have a .500 record at home, the R's will be decided underdogs against the Hub horde, who are coached by the locals' former mentor, Lynn Patrick. To point up the difference in the brand of hockey tonight's rivals have been playing— the Rangers haven't won and the Bruins haven't lost in the last six games for each!

OPPOSITE: SIDELINED BY A FOOT INJURY LATE IN HIS CAREER WITH THE RANGERS, DEAN PRENTICE RELAXES AT HOME WITH HIS WIFE, JUNE, AND THEIR BABY, KELLY LYNN. PRENTICE PLAYED FOR 10 YEARS IN NEW YORK.

43

RANGERS WIN, 5-2; HENRY GETS 4

MARCH 13, 1954

The Red Wings "backed into" their sixth NHL title tonight, clinching the championship even though Camille Henry scored four goals to pace the Rangers to a 5-2 upset.

The title officially remains in Detroit, however, since second-place Toronto also lost, 2-1, to Boston, killing off the Maple Leafs' last possible chance of making up the nine-point deficit.

No team in history has ever won six straight regular-season titles. In fact, aside from the Wings, no team has ever won it more than four times.

Henry was a brilliant performer for the Rangers, who are fighting an uphill battle for the fourth and final playoff berth. They made no headway tonight as the Bruins, by winning, remained three points ahead of the New Yorkers.

Henry scored once in each of the first two periods to help New York to a 3-2 lead and nailed it down with two goals within 33 seconds in the final period, as Detroit's Gordie Howe was sitting out a penalty.

The little winger now has 24 goals for the season. He scored the winning goal at 13:19 of the middle session on a fancy play. He skated from behind Detroit's net and hooked the puck past the sprawling Terry Sawchuk.

OPPOSITE: CAMILLE HENRY, A STAR LEFT WING FOR THE RANGERS IN THE 1950S AND 1960S, BROKE INTO THE NHL IN 1953 WITH NEW YORK AND HAD 279 GOALS AND 249 ASSISTS IN 727 NHL GAMES WITH NEW YORK, CHICAGO AND ST. LOUIS BEFORE HE RETIRED FOLLOWING THE 1969-70 SEASON. HERE, HENRY SHOWS OFF ONE OF HIS BATTLE WOUNDS.

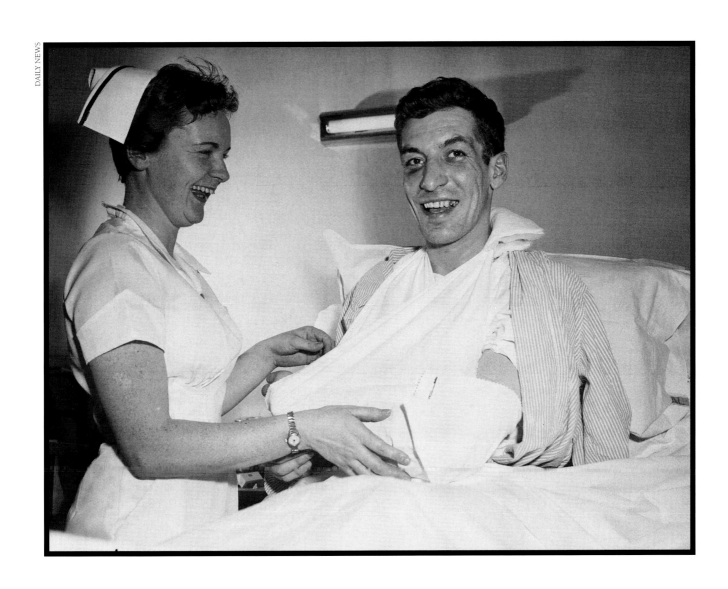

GADSBY NAMED MVP BY RANGERS

MARCH 14, 1956

Although little Gump Worsley was voted the most valuable player in the league halfway through the season, New York's hockey writers yesterday selected Bill Gadsby as the Rangers' MVP in this, his first full season as a Blue.

The offense-minded defenseman, by finishing ahead of the goaltender in a close vote, becomes the 13th winner of the West Side Trophy. He will be presented with a Paul Revere sterling bowl and a $50 savings bond prior to the final game of the season against the Canadiens here Sunday night.

Now in his tenth season in the NHL, although he won't be 29 until August, Gadsby is a leading candidate for All-Star defenseman. He has scored 50 points, and, with 41 assists, is only two shy of the NHL mark for defensemen set last year by Montreal's Doug Harvey. Gadsby has already broken club records for total points and assists by a defenseman.

Gadsby succeeds Danny Lewicki as West Side Trophy winner. Other MVPs, beginning in 1943-44, were Ott Heller and Bryan Hextall (tie), Ab DeMarco, Chuck Rayner, Rayner again, Buddy O'Connor, Edgar Laprade, Laprade-Rayner (tie), Bones Raleigh, Hy Buller, Paul Ronty and Wally Hergesheimer.

OPPOSITE: AFTER BEGINNING HIS CAREER WITH THE CHICAGO BLACKHAWKS, BILL GADSBY WAS TRADED TO THE RANGERS IN 1954. HE WAS NAMED TO THE ALL-STAR TEAM IN EACH OF HIS FIRST FOUR FULL SEASONS IN NEW YORK.

BLUES ZERO BRUINS, 4-0; FONTINATO, FAN TANGLE

BY ASSOCIATED PRESS   MARCH 15, 1958

New York's Andy Bathgate scored his 30th goal, Lou Fontinato was involved in a minor riot and goalie Gump Worsley fashioned an acrobatic shutout today as the Rangers defeated the Bruins, 4-0.

Defenseman Fontinato, in the penalty box for a slashing infraction, was taking a vocal riding from nearby fans and finally began swinging, and quickly, several others joined in a rush which shoved Fontinato against the playing boards.

The New York bench rushed across the ice, and several players hurled themselves into the stands as the Boston bench joined in to help push back the surging crowd. Shortly, the police arrived to separate the humanity and regain control. In the seven-minute delay, one fan in a green sweater was ejected by the police.

Worsley, posting his third whitewash job of the season, made 32 saves against 31 for Boston's Harry Lumley. Perhaps the highlight of Worsley's gymnastic feats came at the end of the second period, when Norm Johnson of the Bruins tipped a Fernie Flaman long shot while crossing in front of Worsley.

Gump, falling to his right, reversed his body in midair, did a handstand and stopped the disk at the goal line with one hand.

Bathgate, one of the NHL's top scorers, got his final tally at 9:31 of the finale after stealing the puck from Allan Stanley behind the Boston nets.

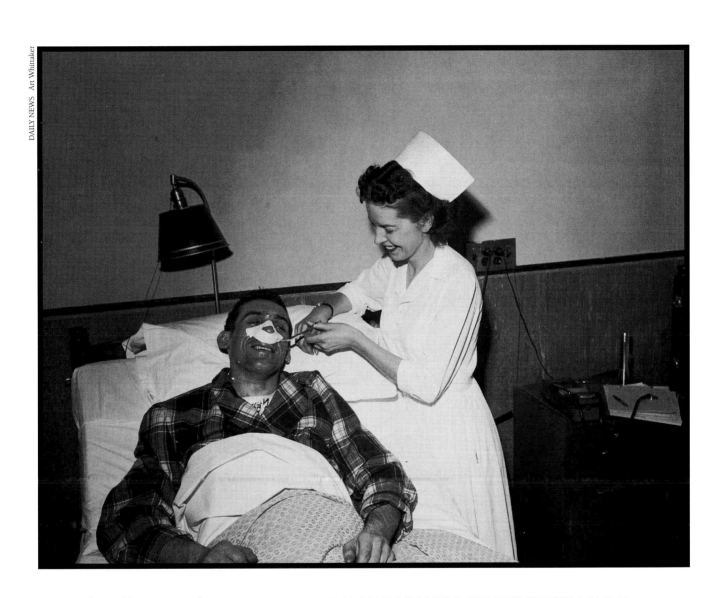

LOU FONTINATO'S HARD-NOSED PLAY PLACED HIM NEAR THE TOP OF THE LEAGUE LIST IN PENALTY MINUTES THROUGHOUT HIS CAREER. HERE, HE IS TREATED FOR A BROKEN NOSE IN MANHATTAN GENERAL HOSPITAL.

BLUES' BATHGATE MVP
BY BIG MARGIN

BY CHRIS KIERAN   MAY 12, 1959

The Rangers went nowhere last season, but you can't prove it by Andy Bathgate. Already named the league's top right-winger by being voted to the '58-'59 All-Star team for the first time, the 26-year-old Bathgate yesterday was given the Hart Trophy as the NHL's Most Valuable Player.

Handy Andy polled 133 points in the split-season balloting, more than double those of Detroit's Gordie Howe, 60, and the Canadiens' Jean Beliveau, 36. He led both sections of the season, earning 67 in the first half and 66 in the second.

Bathgate thus became the third Ranger to win the award and the first since goalie Chuck Rayner in '50; Buddy O'Connor took it in '48.

Playing with a silver plate in his left knee and a brace protecting his right knee, Bathgate finished third in the scoring race behind Montreal's Dickie Moore and Jean Beliveau. He rammed home 40 goals, a Ranger record, and 20% of the team's lamp-lighters for the season, and had 48 assists for a total of 88 points.

Andy made his first appearance with the Blues in 1952-'53, when he showed in 18 games. He didn't score a goal and had only one assist. He went back to Vancouver but returned for 20 games in '53-'54, when he hit for two goals and two assists. He made it to stay in '54-'55 and improved each season with 40 points, 66, 77 and 78.

OPPOSITE: ANDY BATHGATE RANKS THIRD ON THE RANGERS' ALL-TIME SCORING LIST WITH 729 POINTS AND THIRD IN CAREER GOALS (272) AND ASSISTS (457). IN 1958-59, HE WON THE HART TROPHY AS THE NHL'S MOST VALUABLE PLAYER.

RANGERS BLAST BRUINS, 5-2; GUMP SHINES AFTER EYE CUT

BY JIM MCCULLEY   FEBRUARY 6, 1961

The 10,048 hardy souls who let neither snow nor ice keep them from paying their way into the Garden to watch the Rangers play the Bruins last night left the arena rewarded to the hilt. They saw goalie Gump Worsley perform beyond the call of duty and the Blues gain a completely satisfying victory, 5-2, to keep their slim playoff chances alive.

As for the Gumper, he was downright magnificent. Worsley caught a disk in the face early in the game, with the Rangers leading, 1-0. The blow knocked him goofy and damaged him above and below the left eye. But the Gumper wouldn't quit. He left the ice for a 25-minute repair job (two stitches above the eye and one below), returned to the boisterous cheers of his faithful and maintained his shutout until the game had scarcely more than five minutes to go.

Shortly after Worsley came back, the Rangers were back molesting Bruins goalie Bruce Gamble again. Camille Henry tipped in a long pass from Andy Bathgate to make it 2-0 at 8:16, while Boston was a man short. The Rangers gave Gump fine protection for the rest of the period.

Ironically, Worsley actually scored the goal that ended his shutout, although it was credited to forward Charlie Burns. Gump already had stopped Burns' close-up shot. Now he was down on his knees trying to pull the disk in and he did—only with a little too much energy, and then it squirted between his legs and back into the cage.

Dean Prentice drove a shot into an open Boston cage at 6:16 of the second period. After the Rangers killed off a penalty to Harry Howell, Dino got his second of the night, making it 4-0, while the visitors again were shorthanded via a penalty to Zellio Toppazzini.

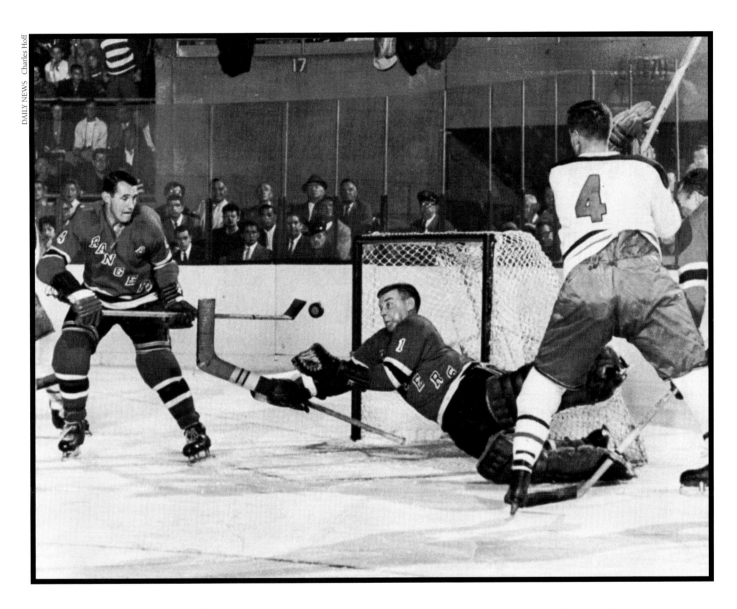

LORNE "GUMP" WORSLEY DEMONSTRATES THE WARLIKE DETERMINATION THAT HE
ALWAYS BROUGHT TO THE ICE. WHILE SAVES LIKE THIS OFTEN CAUSED DAMAGE TO
HIS FACE, WORSLEY'S FEARLESS PLAY EARNED HIM HALL OF FAME HONORS IN 1980.

HARVEY AIMS AT TITLE AS PLAYER-COACH OF BLUES

BY JIMMY POWERS   NOVEMBER 23, 1961

We came in from the course with frozen fingers and wind-reddened faces and the caddy master took us into his shack and poured us a stiff jolt of hot tea laced with Barbados rum. We had given him some hockey tickets. He reported he enjoyed the game, thanks very much, and wasn't Doug Harvey a crackerjack leader?

"It seemed strange looking at Harvey in a New York uniform," he said. "I guess I reacted like most men around here. For years I hated him. He was the man who directed Montreal's rough, tough attack. He put Red Sullivan in the hospital. Now, all of a sudden I love him. I never thought I'd get used to it. But it isn't hard to appreciate his skills, really."

Harvey will be 37 next month, the oldest skater in the National Hockey League, and still one of the best. There is no questioning his importance to the Ranger revival. He has put the club on a sound basis. He commands the respect of the players without being an overbearing shouter.

"The Rangers can do it," Harvey explains, "because essentially they are a good passing team. Sometimes the big job is to get the boys to shoot more instead of taking one pass too many."

High expectations are nothing new to the Rangers' general. No player in the history of hockey has dominated a position the way Harvey has in the last decade. Nine times in the last 10 years he has been picked for the first all-star team. The year he missed he was an alternate.

How does he feel about this season?

"I feel the boys are putting out and that is the main thing. When you are a player-coach you find yourself wondering how the team will react to your own mistakes. After all, I make 'em too. If they take the attitude that if Harvey blows one they can blow one too, then we're in trouble. Fortunately that is not the case. I get the feeling they are trying to make my first year as a coach a good one. If so, we all will wind up with extra money in our pockets."

IN DOUG HARVEY'S FIRST YEAR AS PLAYER-COACH FOR THE RANGERS, HE BECAME THE FIRST-EVER RANGER TO WIN THE NORRIS TROPHY AS THE NHL'S TOP DEFENSEMAN.

PROFESSOR POWERS BLUES OVER BRUINS

BY CHRIS KIERAN   OCTOBER 21, 1963

The big deal Ranger GM Muzz Patrick swung last summer with Montreal had a big payoff in the Garden last night as the Blues jumped to a 4-1 lead against the Bruins before 13,549.

Phil Goyette assisted on four goals in the first period as he fed Andy Bathgate twice and Vic Hadfield and Don McKenney. Johnny Bucyk scored the first goal against Jacques Plante on Garden ice this season in the second session.

The Rangers got right down to business at 1:26 when Hadfield camped on the left side of the net and beat Johnston. He took a feed from Goyette, who put the rubber 10 feet in front of the cage, and he belted home a backhander.

The Bruins came right back and Plante made a neat glove-hand catch of Bolvin's shot from 25-feet out. Cahan got two minutes for holding Gendron at 2:57, but Boston could only get one shot at Plante. That was by Prentice, and the goalie handled it easily.

Goyette took advantage of the Bruins' second penalty of the period with Kurtenbach off for holding Howell. He put a pip on McKenney's weapon, and he had an open cage on the right side at 9:51 to make it 3-0. It was the second power play goal of the season.

OPPOSITE: PHIL "THE PROFESSOR" GOYETTE TIED AN NHL RECORD WITH FOUR ASSISTS IN THE FIRST PERIOD AGAINST THE BRUINS ON OCTOBER 20, 1963.

REG'S MISTAKE PUTS OFFICIAL IN STITCHES

JANUARY 22, 1966

Left-winger Reggie Fleming, traded by Boston to the Rangers 10 days ago for his "muscle," this afternoon hit the wrong man—and not without penalty. In the course of the Bruins' 5-3 victory, the new Blue, in trying to get at Boston's Terrible Teddy Green, inadvertently slashed linesman Brian Sopp above the left eye.

Fleming's slashing act, for which Sopp required five stitches, cost Reggie two minor penalties, a 10-minute misconduct, a game-misconduct and an automatic $75 fine.

It is also a good bet that the newest Ranger faces further action from NHL president Clarence Campbell.

A total of 20 penalties—for 70 minutes—were assessed by referee Frank Udvari in a game that was exceptionally rough from the outset. The Fleming-Green battle didn't take place until the 17th minute of the middle period.

The big Boston defenseman and the just-as-big Ranger forward tangled on the ice and were parted only after Green caught his former teammate with a hard right to the left eye.

Green was already in the penalty box, about to serve two minutes for "roughing," when Fleming attempted to get at him. Sopp, intervening, was slashed and also jammed a hand in the penalty box door.

OPPOSITE: TWO YOUTH HOCKEY PLAYERS LISTEN TO RANGER STANDOUT REGGIE FLEMING. KNOWN FOR HIS PHYSICAL APPROACH TO THE GAME, FLEMING WAS ACQUIRED BY THE RANGERS IN 1966 TO ADD MUCH-NEEDED MUSCLE TO THE TEAM.

Blues End 2-Game Skid on Howell's Big Night

By Dana Mozley   January 26, 1967

Harry "The Horse" Howell scored a famous first last night, becoming the initial Ranger player ever to be honored by a night at the Garden. A standing-room crowd of 15,925 was on hand as Howell received more gifts than Joe DiMaggio and Mickey Mantle received on their Stadium Days a few years ago. The list included a '67 Mercury Cougar, golf equipment, and vacations to Palm Beach and Miami Beach.

Howell, the longtime Ranger defenseman who got his first All-Star award earlier in the day, was focused on helping the Blues defeat Boston at the Garden before sharing the magical evening with his friends, teammates and fans. The Rangers, who hadn't blown three in a row all through this most successful season, were trying to end a two-game slide.

Guaranteeing a magical evening, the Rangers won, 2-1, when Bob Nevin broke a deadlock late in the third period. And guess who, besides Nevin, earned an assist? Harry Howell, of course.

Opposite: Flanked by his parents, Mr. and Mrs. Vernon Howell, and accompanied by his wife, Marilyn, and their children, Cheryl, 11, and Danny, 7, veteran Ranger defenseman Harry Howell expresses his appreciation to fans on "Harry Howell Night." Later, after the game began, Howell was presented with the Rangers' first penalty of the night when he held John Bucyk of the Bruins. Howell was inducted into the Hockey Hall of Fame in 1979.

RATELLE GETS RAVES FROM FANS, FRANCIS

BY LYNN HUDSON   DECEMBER 18, 1970

"Did you see the way Ratelle went in on that goalie and stayed in front of him for about five minutes before he shot?" a fan said after Sunday night's 4-0 Ranger shutout of the Kings. "That's experience, man, real experience."

The fan's admiration was for the way Jean Ratelle had nearly faked Los Angeles goalie Denis DeJordy out of his skates as he went in on him slowly in the second period and scored the third Ranger goal of the evening.

"Ratelle gave DeJordy so many dekes I nearly fell off the bench just watching him," Ranger coach Emile Francis commented about the same play.

Francis is, naturally enough, a Ratelle fan. The handsome, 30-year-old center has scored 32 goals for him in each of the last three seasons.

Jean's goal against Los Angeles was his 14th of this season, and he added his 15th in the third period Wednesday night as the Rangers completed their second consecutive shutout, another 4-0 job, against the Buffalo Sabres.

Wednesday night's game was only the Rangers' 30th of 78 games, so Ratelle is running well head of his 32-goal pace of the last three seasons and appears to be on the way to the most successful year of one of the most consistent careers in the NHL.

Besides his 15 goals, he has 17 assists for 32 points; that's 11 more than any other Ranger. It's the kind of year for which most hockey players would be expecting to pick up a lot of bonus money. And any year before this one, Ratelle would have been, too.

OPPOSITE: JEAN RATELLE, KNOWN FOR HIS GRACE AND CLASS, PLAYED 15 SEASONS WITH THE RANGERS, SETTING A SCORING RECORD IN 1972 WITH 109 POINTS IN 63 GAMES. HIS GREATEST GOAL-SCORING NIGHT OCCURRED ON NOVEMBER 21, 1971, WHEN RATELLE PULLED THE HAT TRICK PLUS ONE.

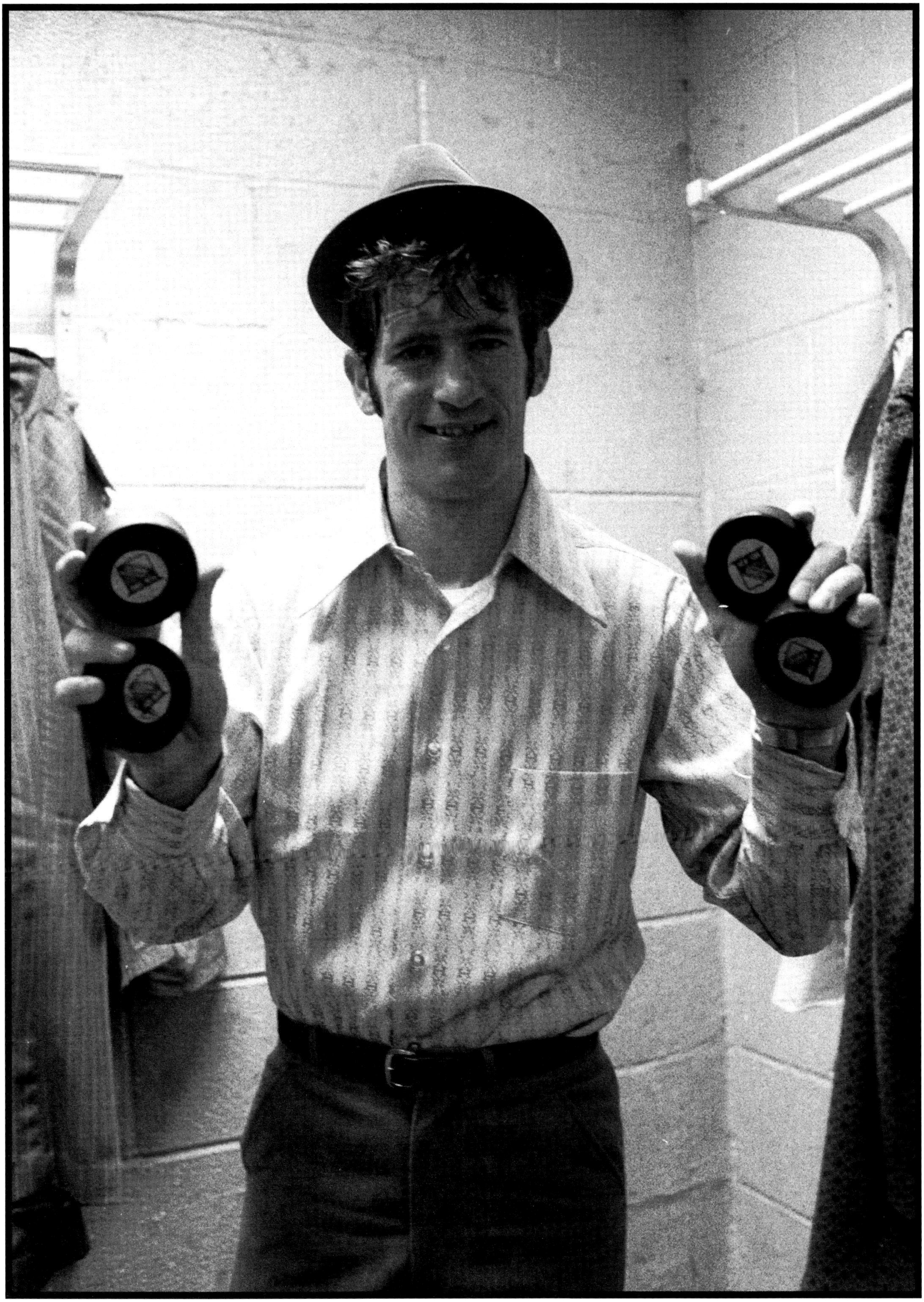
DAILY NEWS Gene Kappock

PARK'S TOPS
WITH RANGERS

BY DANA MOZLEY   JANUARY 11, 1971

First place, Brad Park and the local weather were the main topics of discussion today as the division-leading Rangers began preparations for their Friday night date in Oakland.

The fact that Boston can't do a thing about the Rangers' estate in the standings until the Bruins play the Kings tomorrow night was a source of comfort to the Blueshirts. They also got a good feeling from the fact that Park, their All-Star defenseman, had been named the outstanding performer in recent games here and in St. Louis.

The 22-year-old Park had been brilliant in every respect in the Rangers' sixth straight victory last night, a 4-2 decision over the Canucks that lifted them past the Bruins into first place. Park dominated to the point that some people even felt sorry for him.

One was Big Babe Pratt, the ex-Ranger All-Star defenseman. "In some ways Park is better than Bobby Orr. It's a shame two such outstanding defensemen should come along at the same time and that one, with certain superior offensive skills, should put the other well back in his shadow."

OPPOSITE: BRAD PARK WAS SELECTED TO THE ALL-STAR TEAM SEVEN TIMES IN EIGHT YEARS BETWEEN 1969 AND 1978. DESPITE HIS OUTSTANDING DEFENSIVE PERFORMANCES, PARK NEVER WON THE NORRIS TROPHY, FINISHING AS RUNNER-UP TO BOBBY ORR FOUR TIMES.

VIC HITS 50 AS RANGERS LOSE, 6-5

BY BILL VERIGAN   APRIL 3, 1972

After the Rangers' 6-5 loss to the Canadiens yesterday, Vic Hadfield held the puck that had made him the sixth NHL player in history to score 50 goals in a season.

He had waited until the last 5:14 seconds of the season, and the pressure was almost unbearable, even for him, to get that 50th goal. Now, he grinned and tossed the puck to his 7-year-old son, Jeff, to play with.

The story began with Hadfield needing two goals at the start of the game to match the plateau reached only by Maurice Richard, Bobby Hull, Phil Esposito, John Bucyk and Boom Boom Geoffrion. If he failed, he wouldn't get another chance this season.

The rugged, blond left-winger found his path blocked during the second period and drove the puck across the ice to defenseman Park, who flipped it over to Gilbert on the right side of the net. Hadfield moved toward the net, caught the puck on the move and popped it past DeJordy.

"Until I got that 49th goal, I began to feel the pressure," Hadfield said. "It hadn't been so much before then, but then I began to feel it. The nervousness started to get to me when there was one to go. I knew how important it was."

The nervousness showed. At one point, with the path between him and the puck hopelessly blocked, Hadfield stood waving his arms to attract attention to himself in front of the goal.

And finally, swiftly, the opportunity came, with Jim Neilson passing the puck to Rod Seiling. Another pass to Vic on the left corner, a stick's distance away from DeJordy, and No. 50 was over.

"The last time I heard anything like that (the crowd's three-minute ovation) was when I scored three goals in the playoffs," Hadfield recalled.

A JUBILANT VIC HADFIELD, WHO BECAME THE FIRST RANGER AND ONLY THE SIXTH MAN
IN THE HISTORY OF THE NHL TO TALLY 50 GOALS IN A SEASON, SHOWS OFF PUCKS 49
AND 50.

BRUINS WIN STANLEY CUP, TOP RANGERS

BY NORM MILLER   MAY 12, 1972

The Bruins won their second Stanley Cup championship in the past three seasons when they beat the Rangers, 3-0, at the Garden, clinching the final series, four games to two.

After the Rangers had missed two early power-play opportunities, the Bruins cashed in on a penalty to Walt Tkaczuk for a goal by Bobby Orr, giving them a 1-0 first-period lead.

The bad feeling between the two teams erupted in a fight between Vic Hadfield and Boston's Ken Hodge. Orr shortly drew a 10-minute misconduct for abusing referee Art Skov.

Hodge got the better of his fight with Hadfield a few minutes later. Hadfield, who has been playing with a dislocated right thumb, had to hold back his punches. Both went off with minor penalties and five additional minutes for fighting.

Orr was banished for 10 minutes when he protested Skov's decision to banish both Boston's Wayne Cashman and New York's Gary Doak in a charging, high-sticking duel.

"Mr. Wonderful" was so incensed that he had to be restrained by teammates from resuming his violent complaint to the ref.

With Orr off and both sides playing with four skaters, the Rangers forced the attack. Cheevers kicked out a hard close-in shot by Pete Stemkowski. The Rangers had a 9-8 edge in shots-on-goal during the period.

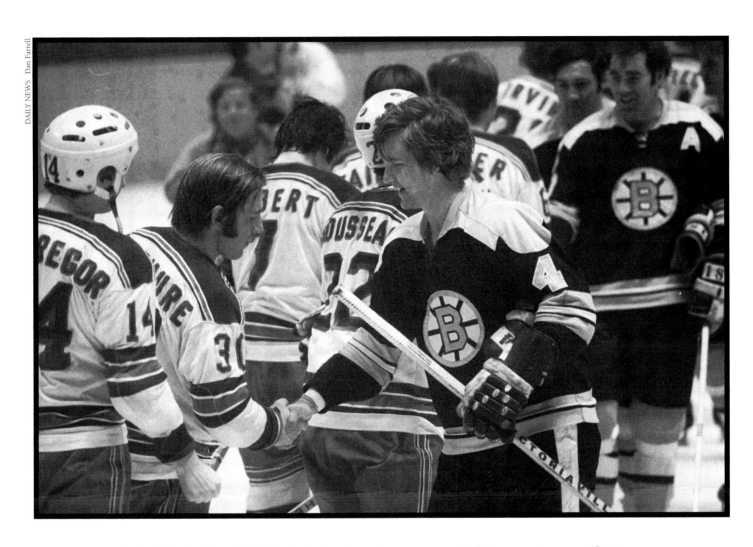

BRUINS ACE BOBBY ORR (RIGHT) SHAKES HANDS WITH RANGERS GOALIE GILLES
VILLEMURE AFTER BOSTON'S 3-0 VICTORY OVER THE RANGERS AT MADISON
SQUARE GARDEN FOR THE STANLEY CUP.

TEARY EDDIE RETURNS, RATTLES RANGERS, 6-4

BY WES GAFFER   NOVEMBER 3, 1975

It was an emotion-packed night for Eddie Giacomin and his former Ranger teammates, the Ranger teammates he had just beaten, 6-4, at the Garden. The goalie, who looked so strange in a red uniform with an unfamiliar No. 31 on the back, fought for breath, words and to keep back the tears that had flowed just before the start of the game.

It was Eddie's night right from the outset. Only six hours earlier, he agreed to terms to play one night at least with the Detroit Red Wings.

The crowd, ignoring the Rangers, roared "Ed-dee, Ed-dee" as Giacomin stepped on the Garden ice. They cheered him all through the 15-minute warm-up. They drowned out the National Anthem with their louder and louder chanting, Giacomin twice giving a slight wave of acknowledgment that each time sent the fans to a higher level of excitement.

"At first I thought it was sweat," Eddie was to say later at an unprecedented, separate-room post-game news conference. "Then I realized it was tears, and I knew the fans at that end of the rink—I know the guys in the press box could see—knew I was crying a bit.

"It was extra hard for them (the Rangers) as much as for me. Lucky I had my mask on (during the game). I could see it in their eyes, and they would have seen tears in mine if it wasn't for my mask. Deep down, I had a funny feeling (about the crowd), if I stepped into the net, they'd be with me."

He laughed wryly. "During the game there was one player, I won't tell you his name, said to me, 'I'm sorry,' and then he scored on me. Four of them did that (score), so you'll have a tough time guessing."

Eddie added that he had no hard feelings toward the team or the Ranger brass. The crowd, an automatic 17,500 did, turning the game into a Red Wings' home game with their cheering.

OPPOSITE: PLAYING HIS FIRST GAME AGAINST THE RANGERS AFTER HE WAS RE-LEASED IN 1975, DETROIT'S EDDIE GIACOMIN WIPES HIS EYES AS HE GETS A STANDING OVATION AT MADISON SQUARE GARDEN.

LATEST STUNNER: ESPOSITO A RANGER

BY WES GAFFER   NOVEMBER 8, 1975

The Rangers, a team in turmoil, engineered a dramatic, five-player trade with the Bruins that brought Phil Esposito, the most explosive scorer in hockey history, to New York.

The price was high: Brad Park, Jean Ratelle and minor leaguer Joe Zanussi to Boston for Esposito and Carol Vadnais, a sturdy defenseman and a crack shot.

Only Zanussi, the AHL's leading scorer at Providence, had to log considerable travel time to join his new team. The Bruins were in Vancover, where they play tonight, and Rangers in Oakland, where they played last night.

The bombshell burst at a hurried news conference called for the Garden at noon time. Ranger GM Emile Francis, who had left St. Louis at 5:30 in the morning to be present, made the announcement with team president Bill Jennings and Mike Burke at the rear of the audience.

As a preamble to the trade announcement, Francis said, "This is my response to the people I work for and the New York fans. It's our ambition to have more than a winning hockey club, to have a championship club."

Speaking of Esposito, the Cat said: "He's the type of hockey player I've always admired, a leader. He lifted the Bruins to two Stanley Cups and the work he did with Team Canada in '72 . . . . He's going to be a leader on this hockey club."

OPPOSITE: IN 1975 THE RANGERS SHOCKED THEIR FANS BY TRADING BRAD PARK AND JEAN RATELLE TO BOSTON FOR PHIL ESPOSITO AND CAROL VADNAIS.

VICKERS SCORCHING, IGNITES RANGERS, 11-4

BY WES GAFFER   FEBRUARY 19, 1976

All that latent violence coach John Ferguson tried to fan into flame burst forth last night at the Garden. The Rangers scored a season-high total of goals in consuming the Washington Capitals, 11-4, three of the goals and four of the assists credited to Steve Vickers, who broke Don (Bones) Raleigh's 21-year-old team record for most points in a game.

Vickers netted the next-to-last goal of the game, at 15:02 of the third period, to set the Ranger record. He did it at left wing, his usual position, but "it was a good thing," Ferguson explained, "because I was going to put him at right wing with (Phil) Esposito on the next shift so he could get his seventh point."

When the goal rattled behind beleaguered Washington goalie Ron Low, the normally phlegmatic Vickers smiled, a fact noted by the customers and empty seats that added up to 17,500. Said modest hero Vickers, "Every game's a playoff game from here on in. I think last night's game (the 3-1 victory over the Islanders) was a key game. Everybody beats Washington."

Leaning back, tired but enjoying the attention, Steve continued: "I'm a ripened veteran (of 24), and I haven't been performing too well, nor am I up to my goal production of the past." His three goals gave him a total of 24 for the season.

"I shaved my mustache Tuesday to get myself and the team some luck. And, for the last three games, (Nick, defenseman) Beverley calls me out of the dressing room before the game and between periods—I'm always the last man the last three games— and it's working. Yeah, I'm superstitious and I'm not going to change anything." Steve knocked wood for emphasis.

OPPOSITE: RANGER STEVE VICKERS WEARS A HAT ON HIS HEAD, A SMILE ON HIS FACE AND FOUR PUCKS ON HIS CHEST AFTER SCORING FOUR GOALS AGAINST WASHINGTON.

RANGERS AX STARS ON GILBERT'S NIGHT

BY LAWRIE MIFFLIN   MARCH 10, 1977

The surprising North Stars had won five of their last seven games coming into the Garden last night, including a triumph over the Islanders the night before. But they never had to compete on Rod Gilbert Night, and the Rangers' charged up feelings after that celebration helped lift them to a 6-4 victory over Minnesota.

The evening began with a two-minute standing ovation for Gilbert, followed by a 20-minute ceremony in honor of the 16-year veteran who is the Rangers' highest all-time scorer. The only other Ranger to be honored with a special night, Harry Howell, was on ice for the festivities, along with former Rangers Brad Park, Jean Ratelle, Vic Hadfield, Andy Bathgate and Camille Henry.

As Gilbert started to speak, he was drowned out by a chant of "Rocky! Rocky!" from the standing-room-only crowd. When he tried again, his face was wet and he was swallowing hard to control his voice.

"My friends," he said. "And I think of all of you here tonight as my friends, . . . you have given me a home, friendship, respect and love . . . all things more important than fame. For these I will always be grateful to you."

OPPOSITE: ROD GILBERT HOLDS THE PUCK THAT HE SHOT PAST BERNIE PARENT FOR THE WINNING GOAL IN A GAME AGAINST THE FLYERS.

SONNY'S $2M START
RANGER BID HIGHEST FOR 2 WHA ACES

BY NORM MILLER   JANUARY 19, 1978

At the enthusiastic urging of Sonny Werblin, the Rangers have offered to make two young Swedes the highest-paid players in hockey if they'll jump from the Winnipeg Jets of the WHA at the end of this season.

Don Baizley, attorney for forwards Anders Hedberg and Ulf Nilsson, confirmed yesterday that the Rangers have offered each player a two-year contract calling for $475,000 a season.

Baizley said this was the highest of the bids the Swedes have received from eight NHL clubs. It topped the next highest, from the Philadelphia Flyers, by $100,000.

Hedberg, 26, and Nilsson, 27, have had spectacular careers since they signed with the WHA Jets in 1974-75. Hockey men say they should do just as well in the NHL.

Hedberg was WHA rookie of the year in 1974-75 and a league all-star in his first three seasons, scoring 53, 50 and 70 goals. Nilsson is more of a playmaker who has been given much credit for Hedberg's 70 regular-season goals last year.

So far this year, Hedberg has 33 goals and 32 assists for 65 points; Nilsson has 16 goals and a league-leading 41 assists.

"We're very hopeful we can sign them," Rangers President Bill Jennings said yesterday. "We consider them world-class hockey players."

OPPOSITE: ANDERS HEDBERG, NEW COACH FRED SHERO AND ULF NILSSON POSE AT MADISON SQUARE GARDEN. THE TWO PLAYERS SIGNED FOR $2.4 MILLION FROM THE BLUESHIRTS OVER TWO YEARS.

THE GREEN LIGHT TOLD THE STORY

BY MIKE LUPICA   MAY 9, 1979

There were less than 10 seconds left now, and the wild noise of the countdown was tumbling crazily down from everywhere, trailed by confetti and white balloons, getting louder as it moved section by section toward the ice at Madison Square Garden. John Davidson, a mighty goalie, was raising an arm and a big stick into the air, greeting the noise in triumph. Four seconds. Two seconds. The little green light behind Davidson went off as a white balloon bounced off it. The green light meant no more goals could be scored. The green light told that the series between the Rangers and Islanders was over. The Rangers had won it. The Garden screamed its thanks.

It was over. The Railroad Series was over. The Rangers were in the finals of the Stanley Cup, still working hard on their Miracle of Madison Square Garden. Last night was for themselves, and the Islanders, and New York, and the best damn hockey battle the City might ever see.

The Rangers had won the game 2-1. They had won the series 4-2.

The Rangers will go after a Stanley Cup starting Saturday, against either the Montreal Canadiens or the Boston Bruins. New York will raise itself up for that little chase, because the City becomes a little excited when there is a championship in sight.

Sports fans in New York are going to feel differently about hockey for a long time because of the show the Rangers and Islanders gave us. Maybe it is better to call it a gift.

It is the way the Rangers went after the favored Islanders that made it big. They never let up, never let their balloon burst. Cynics kept looking for signs that this was all a fluke; there were never any signs. The Rangers were going to win this thing.

OPPOSITE: AFTER CLINCHING THE 1979 "RAILWAY" SERIES AGAINST THE ISLANDERS, RANGER STAR PHIL ESPOSITO SAID, "FOR TWO WEEKS, I HAVEN'T BEEN ABLE TO WALK DOWN THE STREET WITHOUT SOMEBODY STOPPING ME, WANTING TO TALK ABOUT THIS. WHAT WE DID HERE WILL ALWAYS BE REMEMBERED IN NEW YORK."

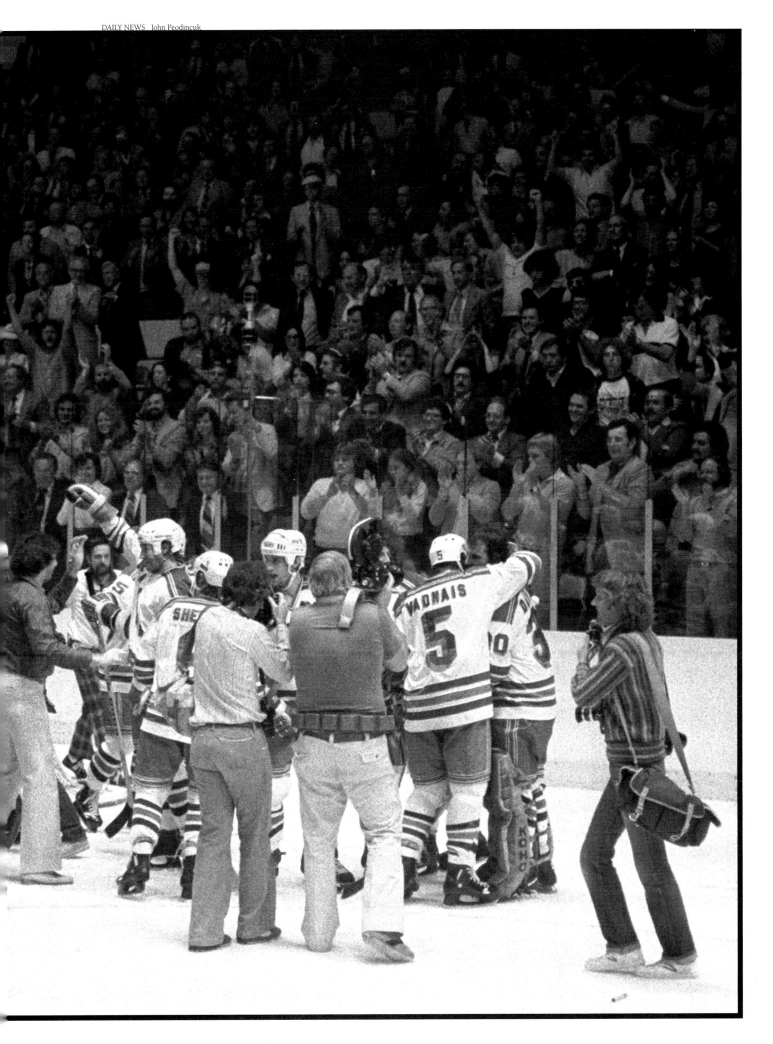

DUGUAY TAKES PLAY TO NEXT LEVEL

BY JIM NAUGHTON   MARCH 6, 1980

Anders Hedberg, the Rangers' right wing, has a friend who recently worked as a hostess in Charley O's, the restaurant adjacent to Madison Square Garden. On the day of Rangers games, she told Hedberg, the phone starts to ring early. The subject of conversation is usually Ron Duguay.

"All these young girls," said Hedberg, "would call up and say, 'I've got to sit near Doogie. Oh, I'm in love with Doogie. Please let me sit near Doogie.'"

For whatever reason—looks, style, performance—Duguay, the center-right wing attracts attention.

Over the last few weeks, Duguay has become one of the more important Rangers. He was the chief reason the president of Madison Square Garden Corporation, Sonny Werblin, vetoed a recent trade with Toronto. He is a favorite with fans, espe-cially females, and in the last month he has been playing his best hockey of an other-wise mediocre season.

After last night's game, Duguay had scored five goals in his last five games.

At 6 feet 2 inches and 210 pounds, with impressive skating speed, he has the mak-ings of a star. Coach Fred Shero has given him more ice time recently and has used him to kill penalties.

"He's a big kid," Shero said of the 22-year-old Duguay. "He can take the extra work. He's been playing much better lately."

Duguay says he is a victim of his image. "I look like a playboy," he said. "That's what people think."

Duguay attributes his recent success to hard work and some luck. "The more I play, the better I feel." he said. "I'm just getting some breaks, that's all."

DESPITE HIS CHRONIC "PLAYBOY" IMAGE, RON DUGUAY WAS A STANDOUT PLAYER FOR THE RANGERS. IN THE 1979-80 PLAYOFFS. DUGUAY SCORED FIVE GOALS AND HAD TWO ASSISTS IN NINE GAMES.

VANBIESBROUCK WINS DEBUT, 2-1

BY FRANK BROWN   DECEMBER 6, 1981

John Vanbiesbrouck recorded the victory he had promised in his first NHL game last night. The 18-year-old Detroit native, the youngest goalie ever to start a game for the Rangers in their 56-year history, gave up a first-period goal but was perfect from there in boosting New York to a 2-1 triumph over the Colorado Rockies.

"Predicting the victory was just part of the game. You always have to think positive," said the 5-8, 170-pound Vanbiesbrouck, who had said Friday he would win. "But the best thing about this is proving to the guys in this room that I can stop the puck in the NHL. You let them know you can play, and they don't have to worry about you. They have enough to worry about."

Though the Rockies scored first, when Paul Gagne potted a 25-footer at 13:11 of the first period, a shorthanded tally by Mark Pavelich and a tip-in by Jere Gillis gave Vanbiesbrouck the lead he needed.

Vanbiesbrouck showed the poise of a far more experienced goalie. His best save of all came on MacMillan, who swept around the right wing after defenseman Tom Laidlaw had fallen. Vanbiesbrouck held his ground and dropped to his knees to stop the veteran wing.

The youngster added a quick blocker stop on a Bob Lorimer shot with 8:03 to play, and though the Rockies did what they could, the performance of Vanbiesbrouck, who stopped 29 shots, was just too much last night.

It was the first time in 11 games the Rangers had held an opponent to one goal.

OPPOSITE: RANGERS' GOALIE JOHN VANBIESBROUCK HELD THE COLORADO ROCKIES TO ONE GOAL IN HIS DEBUT IN THE NHL. VANBIESBROUCK WOULD GO ON TO BECOME ONE OF THE WINNINGEST GOALIES IN NHL HISTORY.

KISIO BURNS DEVILS

BY JIM PORIS   DECEMBER 27, 1986

So what, the Devils came back from a lost cause. They're very good at that. It makes for great excitement and great copy about big hearts and character.

But lately they're always finding something to come back from. Last night, it was another four-goal Ranger blitz in the first period, highlighted by Kelly Kisio's first NHL hat trick. That was too much ground to make up.

So now the fourth-place Devils find that the fifth-place Rangers have erased four points of a six-point deficit after sweeping the home-and-home set with a 7-4 triumph at the Meadowlands Arena.

The Rangers clinched it early, jumping to a 4-0 lead. The game was 38 seconds old when Kisio beat Devils' starter Kirk McLean through a screen. At 4:46, he netted Ron Greschner's blocked shot on the power play. Tomas Sandstrom split Bruce Driver and

Claude Loiselle to chip the third goal past McLean at 6:21. And Kisio potted his second power-play tally during a two-man advantage at 9:36 to complete his trick, beating Alain Chevrier, who had replaced McLean after the third goal.

"It's just one of those things where everything goes right," said Kisio. "You get the adrenaline going, and everyone says you're hot, 'Shoot'—and when you do everything goes in."

The Rangers now have played five games of the 10-game stretch in which they play Patrick Division rivals seven times. And they have won four of those games— beating New Jersey and Washington twice, losing to the Isles.

The end of the year is closing fast on the Devils. The Rangers are making noise already.

KELLY KISIO OF THE RANGERS CELEBRATES A GOAL AT MADISON SQUARE GARDEN. KISIO SCORED HIS FIRST NHL HAT TRICK AGAINST NEW JERSEY ON DECEMBER 26, 1986.

BACK 'HAT' IN HAND, SANDSTROM HELPS SINK ISLES

BY FRANK BROWN   MARCH 5, 1987

Something got the Rangers mad. Something got them hungry. Something or someone, defenseman Willie Huber said, told them "That we better smarten up and play better hockey."

Perhaps it was the return from a nine-game absence of Tomas Sandstrom, who merely set a Rangers record by scoring three times—including the 6-3 winner with 11:01 to play and the 7-5 rally-killer with 3:03 left.

Prior to the game, in his stall near the far wall, a quiet Sandstrom geared himself to play—just three weeks after spraining his ankle and chipping off a piece of bone in Quebec against the Soviets.

"It was tough to get control of the puck, tough to skate with it," Sandstrom said. "I was almost dead after the first period."

Well, it was Sandstrom's ghost, then, who decided the game in the third with his second and third goals of the match—the ones that gave the Rangers a club-record 10 individual performances of three or more goals this season.

"It's a relief to have him back," said Sandstorm's center, Walt Poddubny. "He opens ice for me. Instead of them just having one guy to concentrate on (Poddubny), the other team has two guys to worry about."

"He's got so much confidence in himself, he wants to play so bad. He loves to play so much," Phil Esposito said. "If he continues to keep himself mentally fit like he has—playing that sharp after that long a layoff—there's no telling what he can do."

OPPOSITE: THE RANGERS' TOMAS SANDSTROM (RIGHT) CELEBRATES WITH TEAM-MATE JAN ERIXON AFTER SANDSTROM SCORED A HAT TRICK. SANDSTROM SCORED 40 GOALS AND A TEAM-RECORD FOUR HAT TRICKS IN THE 1986-87 SEASON, DE-SPITE BREAKING HIS ANKLE EARLY IN THE SEASON.

RANGERS' BECK
EXITS A WINNER

BY FRANK BROWN   OCTOBER 15, 1987

Winning is invoked as the bottom line whenever coaches are hired and fired. Applying that same measuring stick to Barry Beck's NHL career—which officially ended with the announcement of his retirement—leads to a simple conclusion: The Rangers have lost a winner.

The 30-year-old defenseman with the ruined left shoulder will be remembered by some fans as a quitter for sitting out last season. Beck will be remembered by others as the player branded with the tag of "savior," who never quite reached that potential and never led the Rangers to a championship.

But there is another bottom line that expresses as much as the bodychecks he threw, as much as the big slap shots he took. It says: in the seven full regular seasons he spent with them, the Rangers were a .523 team when Beck was in their lineup and a .444 team when he wasn't.

"I've obviously decided to retire and to move on to another career, whatever that may be," he said. "I've been in a pretty big hole (emotionally) for the last week and a half . . . I'm very happy I had a chance to play here . . . All I can say to the fans is, 'thank you.' . . . I was proud of myself for coming back and giving it another shot. I looked at it as being like gambling: sometimes you win, sometimes you lose."

Added Beck's good friend, Pierre Larouche, "It's got to hurt him in his heart that he has to leave because of injury—not because he doesn't want to play anymore. He went away (last season) because of his shoulder. We know that now."

"I'm sure he has had dreams and goals when it comes to hockey. When you reach the age of 30, I think it's not so much personal goals as team goals you think about," Ron Duguay said. "You want to be part of a team that wins a Stanley Cup, and for him to come back after taking a year off, I'm sure he really had it in his mind to be part of that team."

OPPOSITE: THE RANGERS' BARRY BECK (FOREGROUND) AND JOHN DAVIDSON CONTROL THE PUCK. A SHOULDER INJURY FORCED BECK TO RETIRE IN 1987 AFTER SEVEN SEASONS WITH THE RANGERS.

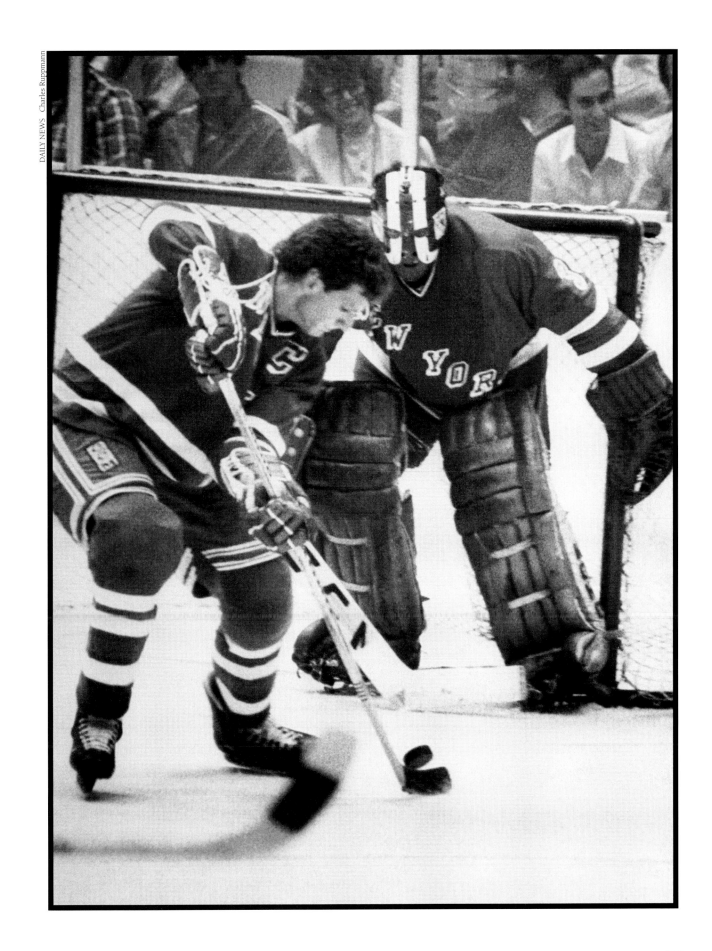

DIONNE PUTS NO. 700 IN BOOKS

NOVEMBER 2, 1987

Marcel Dionne's goal against the Islanders was truly one for the books.

"It's something you try to teach young players," the Rangers' center said after scoring his 700th goal Saturday night in an 8-2 loss to the Islanders. "It's the kind of shot that works.

"It is not a shot that is hard, but it has to be on net. If you hit the goalie in the pads like that when he's moving, then five times out of 10 it's going to go in."

Few others have done it better. He's currently in his 17th season in the NHL and has an option for another year on his contract and figures to fulfill that, too.

"I have tried to be consistent, to go out there and do it every night," Dionne said.

"I tried to be prepared everytime I went out on the ice."

Consistency has been the hallmark of Dionne's career. In a 12-year period with the Los Angeles Kings before he joined the Rangers in a trade last season, Dionne scored at least 50 goals six times. On seven other occasions, he scored no less than 36 goals with the Kings and Detroit Red Wings, his first NHL team.

Dionne started the season needing just seven goals to reach the 700-goal mark. Coming into the 1987-88 season, Dionne had 693 goals and 990 assists for 1,683 points to rank him only behind Howe's 1,850.

THE RANGERS' MARCEL DIONNE RAISES HIS STICK IN CELEBRATION AFTER SCORING A GOAL THAT TIED HIM WITH PHIL ESPOSITO AS THE SECOND ALL-TIME LEADING SCORER IN NHL HISTORY IN FEBRUARY 1988.

EDDIE NO. 1
RANGER OF ALL

BY FRANK BROWN   MARCH 16, 1989

Phil Esposito wasn't exactly sure where he was when he learned the news; he simply recalls his astonishment.

"I just remember being very surprised," Esposito said. "I mean they moved Eddie Giacomin! He *was* the New York Rangers, as far as we were concerned."

The "we" to whom Esposito referred were the Bruins, the team for which Esposito was playing when the Rangers placed Giacomin on waivers and the goalie was claimed by Detroit on October 31, 1975.

Esposito's shock would be replaced by the shock of his own departure barely a week later, November 5, when he was traded to the Rangers. As luck would have it, Esposito would conclude his career with the Rangers and become general manager.

One of the first things Esposito did was bring Giacomin back to the Rangers; one of the most recent Esposito moves was sponsoring the night the Rangers gave Giacomin at the Garden.

"Coming into the Garden and hearing 'Ed-dee, Ed-dee' all the time, it would kind of unnerve you," Esposito said. "We'd say to each other, 'Hey, we can put the puck past this guy. What's the big deal?' But then, the louder they cheered, the harder we'd try to do it and the less we'd get done."

That was part of the Giacomin magic that everyone came to relive as the Rangers retired the No.1 Giacomin wore with such distinction for 538 of his 539 games as a Ranger.

OPPOSITE: HALL OF FAMER EDDIE GIACOMIN SALUTES THE SELLOUT CROWD AT MADISON SQUARE GARDEN AS HIS NO. 1 JERSEY IS RETIRED TO THE RAFTERS.

SMITH TAKES RANGERS' REINS

BY FRANK BROWN   JULY 18, 1989

After sitting dead in the water for more than seven weeks, the Rangers front office finally started moving forward again yesterday when Neil Smith officially was named GM.

"I'll find out the true meaning of 24 hours a day, seven days a week," Smith said after being introduced by Garden sports boss Jack Diller at a Felt Forum news conference. "If I can keep myself stockpiled on coffee, I won't have any handicap at all."

Joe Bucchino, who had conducted the Rangers' amateur draft and had served as interim GM during the 54 days Diller and Garden president Dick Evans searched for Phil Esposito's successor, will remain in the organization as Smith's assistant.

The decision finally was announced just 53 days before the official start of training camp. During the search, Diller and Evans worked from a list of what Evans said was 30 candidates at the outset. Smith caught their eyes early as "one of the rising stars of the league," as Diller put it, but was not free to speak with the Rangers until June 22 and was not hired until Saturday.

"According to Jack Diller, according to Dick Evans, I *was* the top choice," Smith said. "For them to continue the process of being as thorough as they were only makes me convinced I was the right man."

OPPOSITE: UNDER THE LEADERSHIP OF GM NEIL SMITH, THE RANGERS BROUGHT THE STANLEY CUP BACK TO MADISON SQUARE GARDEN IN 1994. SMITH'S SUCCESS HAS EARNED HIM NUMEROUS EXECUTIVE OF THE YEAR AWARDS AND A PROMOTION TO TEAM PRESIDENT. HERE, HE'S SHOWN INTRODUCING THE RANGERS' NEW GAME JERSEY IN 1997.

WATSON HAS FOND MEMORIES OF LAST CUP TEAM

BY WAYNE COFFEY   NOVEMBER 12, 1989

A HALF CENTURY AGO, on an April night in Maple Leaf Gardens, Dutch Hiller of the New York Rangers dug hard into the corner. "I can remember it as though it were yesterday," Hiller says, recalling The Rangers' 1940 Stanley Cup championship series against Toronto.

He muscled the puck onto his stick and whipped it behind the net. Phil Watson was waiting. "It was a fast kind of play, just like that," Watson says.

The score at the time was 2-2, two minutes into overtime, Game 6 of the Stanley Cup finals. The Rangers lead the series, 3-2. They had taken the first two games at Madison Square Garden, but then the circus came to town and the Rangers were evicted, the balance of the series shifting to Toronto.

Watson reacted instantly, sliding the puck to Bryan Hextall, a left-shooting right wing who led the league with 24 goals that year. "He came burning in like an elephant," Watson says. Hextall snapped it backhanded, high and hard toward the upper right corner. Toronto goaltender Turk Broda made his move but couldn't catch up, and the red light went on and that was it. In an instant the Rangers were hollering and hugging.

Watson was a peppery, fiercely competitive sort. Today, at 75, his language is still colorful. A Montreal native, he was a bona fide character, a French-speaking man known for mangling English. "When I got to New York all I knew how to say was ham and eggs and steak," he says. "So that was all I ate."

OPPOSITE: A MAINSTAY ON THE RANGERS' GREAT EARLY TEAMS, PHIL WATSON MAY HAVE HAD HIS BEST SEASON IN 1941-42, WHEN HE LED THE RANGERS IN ASSISTS (37) AND WAS FOURTH IN THE LEAGUE IN SCORING. HE FINISHED HIS CAREER WITH 127 GOALS AND 233 ASSISTS.

NICHOLLS +2 NETS MESSIER

BY FRANK BROWN   OCTOBER 5, 1991

Mark Messier sat in the far corner of the dressing room at the Forum chatting quietly with Adam Graves as equipment man Tim Paris opened the equipment bags and prepared the team's gear for practice. At each player's place, Paris placed a colorful jersey, and you had to read the team name on the sweater's chest to remind yourself that a fairly remarkable thing had happened yesterday—that the deal had finally gone through, that Mark Messier is a Ranger now.

Messier arrived, along with unspecified future considerations, in exchange for center Bernie Nicholls, right wing Steven Rice and left wing Louie DeBrusk. He arrived with five Stanley Cup rings, one regular-season MVP award, one playoff MVP, three first-team All-Star selections and one Lester Pearson Award as Canada's top male athlete.

And the Rangers, to a man, were overjoyed.

"It was a fantastic 12 years (in Edmonton), but I'm looking more than forward to the new challenge ahead of me," Messier said. "I'm starting a so-called 'second career.'"

In his "first" career, Messier vaulted to world-class prominence. He produced 392 goals and 1,034 total points in just 851 games while proving one of the game's fiercest competitors and staunchest leaders.

"I don't think there's any guy who wants to win more than Mark Messier," Graves said.

OPPOSITE: SUPERSTAR MARK MESSIER CAME TO THE RANGERS IN A 1991 BLOCKBUSTER TRADE WITH EDMONTON THAT SENT THE RANGERS' BERNIE NICHOLLS, STEVEN RICE AND LOUIE DEBRUSK TO THE OILERS.

LARMER MAKES GREAT FIRST IMPRESSION AND FIRST GOAL

BY FRANK BROWN   NOVEMBER 4, 1993

Steve Larmer was everything Mike Keenan said he would be. In his Rangers debut at the Garden last night, the right wing was gritty and smart, an earnest hard worker who finished his checks, went to the net and contributed the winning goal to his new team's 6-3 dismissal of the Vancouver Canucks.

"I can't remember being this nervous in a long time," Larmer said. "A little emotion and excitement can help you a lot."

An excited Larmer looks about the same as Larmer depressed. You kind of have to take his word for it.

"Everybody has made me feel real comfortable," said the veteran, obtained from Chicago via Hartford Tuesday on the deal that made Whalers of James Patrick and Darren Turcotte.

"This is a really talented team. I think it's going to go a long way, and we're going to have a lot of fun doing it."

OPPOSITE: DURING THE 1994-95 SEASON, STEVE LARMER (CENTER) PLAYED IN HIS 1,000TH NHL GAME AND SCORED HIS 1,000TH CAREER POINT. HERE LARMER IS PRESENTED WITH A RANGER AWARD BY TEAMMATES BRIAN LEETCH (LEFT) AND ADAM GRAVES IN RECOGNITION OF HIS ACCOMPLISHMENTS.

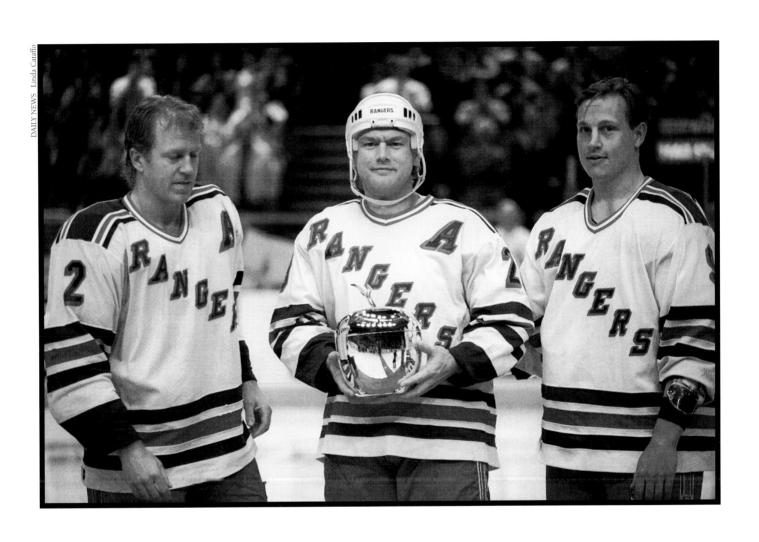

GARTNER JOINS ELITE CLUB AS RANGERS ROLL

BY FRANK BROWN   DECEMBER 27, 1993

More striking than the play, more striking than the pass Alexei Kovalov made for the shot Mike Gartner made just a few feet from the net, was the Garden noise that followed it at 6:16 of the third period last night. Shrill shrieking hurt your ears, unless you were Mike Gartner and you just had made a small group one player larger by scoring the 600th goal of your career.

Gartner saw the puck behind Chris Terreri, sitting in the Devils' net, and instantly his hands went up toward the arena's spiked ceiling—as did his gaze. It was the seventh Ranger goal in an 8-3 triumph, a who-cares goal, really, as far as the outcome was concerned. As far as Gartner and the Rangers were concerned, though, it was the moment a threshold was crossed.

Gordie Howe scored more goals, 801, than Gartner, Wayne Gretzky has scored more. Marcel Dionne and Phil Esposito both had more than 700, and Bobby Hull, fifth on the all-time list, had 610. Gartner was just a bit behind them last night, when he brought the 599-goal total to the Garden. But somehow that shot brought him so much closer.

It may not even have been a shot. Kovalev carried up the left side and Gartner went to the net and Ken Daneyko dived on his belly to try to break up the play. He may have sent the puck past Terreri, but there wasn't a soul in the building who would make that claim. Referee Paul Stewart, unsure if Gartner had kicked in the puck, called for a video review to make sure Gartner's 600th goal had legally scored.

And when the word came down that it was, the Garden noise sounded again and the Ranger bench emptied. Stewart could have called a penalty for delay of game, but he did not. These moments do not occur often.

MIKE GARTNER (SECOND FROM LEFT) CELEBRATES ONE OF HIS MORE THAN 700 CAREER
GOALS, 173 OF WHICH HE SCORED DURING HIS FIVE SEASONS WITH THE RANGERS.

51ST FOR GRAVES IS RANGER MARK

BY FRANK BROWN   MARCH 24, 1994

While the eyes of the hockey world focused on the Great Western Forum to see Wayne Gretzky pass Gordie Howe's career goal record of 801, the eyes of 14,186 at Northlands Coliseum watched as Adam Graves passed Vic Hadfield's one-season Ranger record of 50. And when the left wing did it by launching an off-balance shot under the crossbar from just outside the goalmouth at 17:26 of the first period, the folks here treated Graves as one of their own.

Which, of course, he was.

Graves, the free agent the Oilers wouldn't sign in 1991, became the top single-season goal scorer in Ranger history with his 51st goal in last night's 5-3 Ranger victory. It isn't much by the standards of Gretzky's record 92 goals or even the 76 Alexander Mogilny got for Buffalo last season. But by Ranger standards, remember this was the 4,524th game in the team's 69 seasons, Graves became only the second to produce as many as 50 goals.

"I've got 10 (goals) off my feet, 10 off my butt," said Graves. "I've gotten some of the ugliest goals you've ever seen."

The 50th, though, was lovely for its poetry. At Boston Garden on May 24, 1990, Mark Messier put the Stanley Cup in Graves' hands. On the Northlands pond last night, Messier led a two-on-one up the right side, knowing Graves would join him on the left.

Messier made the perfect backhand pass, which he virtually always does, and Graves put it away, which he has done so many times this season. His one-timer from 15 feet that soared over the dive of goaltender Bill Ranford clanked in under the crossbar, and Hadfield's 22-year-old record was tied.

OPPOSITE: ADAM GRAVES' RECORD-BREAKING 1993-94 SEASON NOT ONLY HELPED LIFT THE RANGERS TO THEIR FIRST STANLEY CUP CHAMPIONSHIP IN 54 YEARS, IT ALSO NETTED HIM HIS FIRST NHL ALL-STAR APPEARANCE AND EARNED HIM NUMEROUS POSTSEASON AWARDS, INCLUDING HIS THIRD STRAIGHT RANGERS MVP HONOR.

LEETCH GOAL IS ANSWER TO GLORY'S CALL

BY JOHN GIANNONE   MAY 10, 1994

Carpe diem. Seize the day.

That's just what Brian Leetch did last night in a series-clinching 4-3 victory over the Capitals. And he did it just in the nick of time for the Rangers.

The game—and the Rangers' suddenly shaken confidence—were hanging in the balance. Leetch seized control of the Rangers' fate and carried his club to its first semifinal appearance in eight years with what, by normal standards would be described as an utterly remarkable goal.

But we all know Brian Leetch is no normal hockey player. Witness his three assists that preceded the dramatic moment. And witness the events leading up to the game-winner with 3:28 remaining.

Leetch took a wobbly pass from Sergei Zubov, which he had to stop and control using a combination of his stick and his left skate. He then made the puck sit flat on the ice, cruised toward Capital goalie Rick Tabaracci and looked for an opening. Leetch waited and waited and then flipped a wrist shot that skidded between Tabaracci's legs. Leetch's goal clinched the series, allowing the Rangers to advance to a showdown with the neighboring Devils.

"You're looking for your biggest players to be their best and come up with the big play," coach Mike Keenan said. "Brian served up the biggest play of his playoff career."

OPPOSITE: IN BRIAN LEETCH'S FIRST SEASON WITH THE RANGERS (1988-89), HE EARNED THE CALDER CUP AS THE NHL'S TOP ROOKIE. HE WENT ON TO WIN THE NORRIS TROPHY AS THE NHL'S BEST DEFENSEMAN IN 1992, AND BROKE THE 100-POINT MARK, A FIRST FOR A RANGER REAR GUARD. IN THE 1994 PLAYOFFS, HE WON THE CONN SMYTHE TROPHY FOR PLAYOFF MVP WHILE HELPING THE RANGERS WIN THE STANLEY CUP.

GUARANTEED! TRUE TO HIS WORD, MESSIER FORGES GAME 7

BY JOHN GIANNONE   MAY 26, 1994

Mark Messier knows that talk is cheap. But in one scintillating, almost mind-boggling 20-minute performance against the Devils, Messier turned his daring pearls of wisdom into priceless works of art. And in the process, Messier was transformed from mere superstar to New York Hockey icon.

Messier, who one day earlier had guaranteed a Ranger victory in this do-or-die game 6, single-handedly put his money where his mouth is with a legendary third-period display. He scored three times, erased a third-period deficit and lifted the Rangers from their very graves to a most amazing 4-2 triumph at Meadowlands Arena.

"I don't think the (earlier) statements meant anything more than getting the team back the confidence they had all year," Messier said. "I needed to let everyone know we could come in here and win. But no one man can win a game or a championship. This is a team sport."

Messier's nick-of-time heroics set up a Game 7 showdown at the Garden, with the winner fighting the Canucks for the right to win the Stanley Cup.

Messier began his superhuman third period and pulled the Rangers even at 2:48 when he grabbed new linemate Alexei Kovalev's pass down the middle, dashed toward the right post and flipped a low backhander into the short side of the net past Martin Brodeur.

Messier and Kovalev teamed again with 7:48 left in the third in what could become the biggest goal in Ranger history. With the teams skating 4-on-4, Messier overpowered Bernie Nicholls in front to bang home a Kovalev rebound and remarkably put the Rangers ahead. Finally, with the Devils on a power play, Messier grabbed John MacLean's stray centering pass and flipped a 170-foot clear that, naturally, skidded directly into the middle of the open net with 1:45 remaining.

"Anytime an athlete does what Mark did, what someone like Muhammad Ali used to do, which is make a bold statement and back it up, that's just outrageous and incredible," Rangers GM Neil Smith said. "This was one of those nights you mark on your calendar, one you never forget. Mark's career will forever be marked by this night."

A FREQUENT SIGHT FOR RANGER FANS—MARK MESSIER CELEBRATING ONE OF HIS GOALS. DURING THE RANGERS' 1993-94 RUN TO THE STANLEY CUP CHAMPIONSHIP, MESSIER LED THE TEAM WITH 12 PLAYOFF GOALS, INCLUDING HIS REMARKABLE THREE-GOAL THIRD PERIOD AGAINST NEW JERSEY IN GAME 6 OF THE CONFERENCE FINALS.

RICHTER AN UNSUNG HERO IN DEVILS SERIES

BY BARRY MEISEL   MAY 28, 1994

It wasn't Eddie Giacomin's fish-out-of-water belly flop on the Montreal Forum ice in 1972, or John Davidson's proud hands-over-head celebration after the Rangers vanquished the Islanders as the Garden rocked in '79, but Mike Richter's nifty little jig spoke volumes of the 27-year-old goalie's glee after the Rangers finally eliminated the Devils, 2-1, in double overtime of Game 7.

He was the most important player of the series, too, arguably the series MVP over Mark Messier and Stephane Matteau. He stopped the Devils' first 23 shots, and all eight in the 24:24 of overtime.

Three plays in overtime stood out in Richter's mind:

• At 11:59, Richter came way out to the side boards to play a loose puck. He got it, but fiddled a little too much as Bill Guerin pressured him. Ultimately, he got back to the net without the Devils getting a shot.

"As ugly as it looked, it got the job done," he said.

• At 13:15 of the first OT, Randy McKay and Bobby Holik attacked two-on-one against Jeff Beukeboom. McKay down right wing waited, waited, and then threw a pass toward Holik charging to the net. Richter poked it out of trouble just as Holik got to it.

• At 3:57 of the second OT, Richter made a save on a 30-foot rocket by Stephane Richer. The rebound popped to Richter's left and Richter dove and sticked it aside before Richer could get it.

IN THE 1993-94 SEASON, RANGERS' GOALTENDER MIKE RICHTER LED THE LEAGUE WITH A CAREER-HIGH 42 WINS AND WAS MVP OF THE ALL-STAR GAME. HE HAD 16 PLAYOFF WINS AND FOUR SHUTOUTS ON THE ROAD TO THE STANLEY CUP.

KEENAN'S TEARS OF JOY

BY BARRY MEISEL   JUNE 15, 1994

As the tears flowed, Mike Keenan lifted the Cup and the Garden roared. They roared for a head coach who was hired 14 months ago to win the Stanley Cup . . . and he had won the Stanley Cup.

"I feel pride, just pride," Keenan said in the glow of his most difficult, yet successful, season. "And privileged. It's an unbelievable feeling. I have so much respect for Mark (Messier), we have such a strong relationship."

Messier paid Keenan an even bigger compliment last night during the electric postgame atmosphere. "I just want to say one thing," he began. "Yesterday, Keenan addressed the team for 15 minutes in the dressing room. It was the most powerful, most intense, most emotional moment I've ever seen in my life. He seized control of the team when it had to be done."

When the final buzzer sounded, Keenan looked for his daughter, Gayla, sitting behind the bench.

He thought of the fans, and the long, long season that ended the way it began, with the Rangers talking about the Stanley Cup.

Keenan reiterated that he planned to be the coach of the Rangers next year, "if they'll have me back."

OPPOSITE: AS MIKE KEENAN RAISES THE STANLEY CUP IN CELEBRATION OF ONE OF THE RANGERS' GREATEST TRIUMPHS, LITTLE DID ANYONE KNOW THAT HE WOULD BE DEPARTING FOR ST. LOUIS JUST TWO MONTHS LATER IN A DISPUTE THAT HAD TO BE RESOLVED BY THE COMMISSIONER'S OFFICE.

BANNER NIGHT: CUP DESCENDS

BY FRANK BROWN   JANUARY 21, 1995

It sat on a table, sparkling in the darkness from all the flashbulbs that were firing. As they lowered it from the Garden score-board, the Stanley Cup wore a green halo of laser light, wore a furry robe of light gray fog. It floated slowly, so slowly, toward the circle of Ranger players who studied its descent in mute astonishment.

That night was a night five decades in the making and—who knows?—it could be five decades from a sequel.

So the Rangers fixed it that the night the banner rose to the Garden heavens also would be the night the Cup drifted down from them.

Before the Atlantic Division and regular-season championship banners went up, there were highlights. Before the Eastern Conference championship banner went up, there were highlights. Before The Big One

went up, there were highlights. Then it was time, time for the flag to fly.

There were spotlights and flashbulbs and happy howls from the crowd. Then the flag began its climb, boosted by bellowing cheers, and Beethoven's "Ode to Joy." There were fireworks and cherry bombs from the scoreboard, like the moment MacTavish won that last draw from Pavel Bure. Then Mark Messier had the Cup in the air one more time, bench-pressing it over his shoulders the way the Rangers lifted the city's spirits. Then he took it for one more lap around the Garden ice.

Then the guys with the gloves came out and took the Cup away. The lasers were gone and the fog was gone and the Cup was gone, too—leaving only remarkable memories of a remarkable achievement.

OPPOSITE: THE MOMENT RANGER FANS HAVE BEEN ANTICIPATING FOR 54 YEARS.

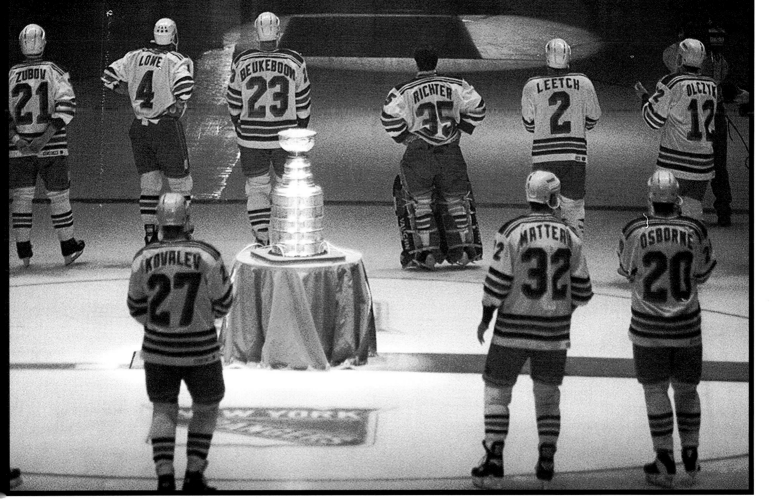

500: MESSIER HAT TRICK MARKS MILESTONE

BY JOHN DELLAPINA   NOVEMBER 7, 1995

The familiar faces in the crowd, the progress of his career, the nature of the game, the needs of his team and even the identity of the opponent had come together to produce a moment that was almost uncanny.

Mark Messier seized it. Because that is what Mark Messier does.

With his Rangers—and make no mistake, they are his—clinging to a one-goal lead in a pivotal game and his incredible body of work one goal short of a magical milestone, Messier steamed down the left side of the Garden ice and loaded his gun for the third time last night. The Rangers' captain fired, found the hole between Rick Tabaracci's goal pads and made the night his own.

The goal, his third of the game, was No. 500 of his Hall of Fame-bound career. It completed his 21st hat trick—the first since his epic guaranteed performance against the Devils—and nailed down a 4-2 victory against his longtime nemesis, the Calgary Flames.

"It's nights like these when you want to

pinch yourself and say, 'I'm a better person and player for him having been around here,'" goaltender Mike Richter said. "When he got here (in 1991), he came with such a great reputation that you began to wonder whether he was more than just a player and a guy. But then he started to do all these things and your suspicions were confirmed: He is more than just a player and a normal person. He's the greatest leader I've ever seen."

That is exactly what Rangers president Neil Smith said he was getting when he traded Bernie Nicholls, Stephen Rice and Louie DeBrusk to Sather's Edmonton Oilers for Messier.

"What a way to get your 500th goal—with a hat trick, at home, against the team that has been your closest nemesis for years. And it's a tremendous accomplishment for a player who is so much more than a goal scorer," Smith said.

"It just all worked out perfectly," Messier said.

It was hardly the first time.

MARK MESSIER CELEBRATES HIS 500TH CAREER GOAL AND HIS THIRD OF THE GAME
IN THE RANGERS' 4-2 VICTORY OVER THE CALGARY FLAMES.

WAYNE-GERS

BY JOHN DELLAPINA   JULY 21, 1996

The greatest player in the history of hockey today joins the greatest leader in the game on The Great White Way.

After a one-day whirlwind of negotiations that ended with an agreement in principle late Friday night, the Rangers will announce at a Garden press conference today that they have signed Wayne Gretzky to a free-agent contract.

It reunites The Great One with Rangers captain Mark Messier eight years after Gretzky was traded from the Edmonton Oilers to the Los Angeles Kings.

Clearly, Messier's dream of playing with his close friend again had some bearing on the Rangers' pursuit of the 35-year-old center. Just as clearly, the Rangers' crying need for a playmaker to coax some goals out of underachieving winger Luc Robitaille prompted the move—although Gretzky and Robitaille had an acrimonious parting two years ago.

It was Gretzky's desire to rejoin Messier and finish his incomparable career in New York that made this dream a reality. Gretzky turned down far more lucrative offers elsewhere this summer—including a two-year, $12.5 million deal to stay in St. Louis and a comparable pact to play in Vancouver.

OPPOSITE: IN 1996, WAYNE GRETZKY HEADED TO NEW YORK FOR A REUNION WITH CLOSE FRIEND AND FORMER EDMONTON TEAMMATE MARK MESSIER. HERE, THE TWO FILM A TV COMMERCIAL IN MANHATTAN.

WAYNE, IT'S BEEN GREAT

BY JOHN DELLAPINA   APRIL 17, 1999

From the beginning, it was always his vision that made him special—his ability to see more clearly than anyone what was possible on a chaotic sheet of ice.

At age 38, Wayne Gretzky's legs don't move like they once did. And his hands aren't as deft. But his vision remains keen.

And what the greatest player in the history of hockey now sees quite clearly—more so than many of those around him—is that the time has come for him to go. So go he did yesterday by announcing his retirement from the National Hockey League.

Those closest to him had begged him not to go through with it—to come back for one last glorious season in which proper good-byes could be said, round-number statistical milestones (900 goals, 2,000 assists) could be met and a winning final note could be sung.

But they either didn't see what he saw, refused to accept it or chose to ignore it.

He delivered his official retirement ad-dress in his adopted home rink and home-town. And he did it with a press conference he and the Garden's public relations depart-ment conceived, one that hit all the right buttons.

A video synopsis of his incomparable career—from Canada's child prodigy to retiring Ranger—and an eloquently simple introduction from MSG broadcaster John Davidson had Janet Gretzky weeping and the entire Rangers team welling up. Ty and Trevor were on hand to support their dad but Gretzky said his daughter, Paulina, did not want to come "Because she thought she'd cry too much."

"In hockey, in professional sports, like in life, there are highs and lows," Gretzky said, his eyes wide open as usual. "Unfortu-nately, sometimes you have to go to funer-als. But fortunately, sometimes you get to go to weddings and fun parties. To me, this is a party and a celebration. And I look upon these next few days as something to really enjoy."

OPPOSITE: THE GREAT ONE MAKES HIS LAST APPEARANCE IN THE GREATEST HOCKEY ARENA IN THE COUNTRY IN FRONT OF THE GAME'S GREATEST FANS.

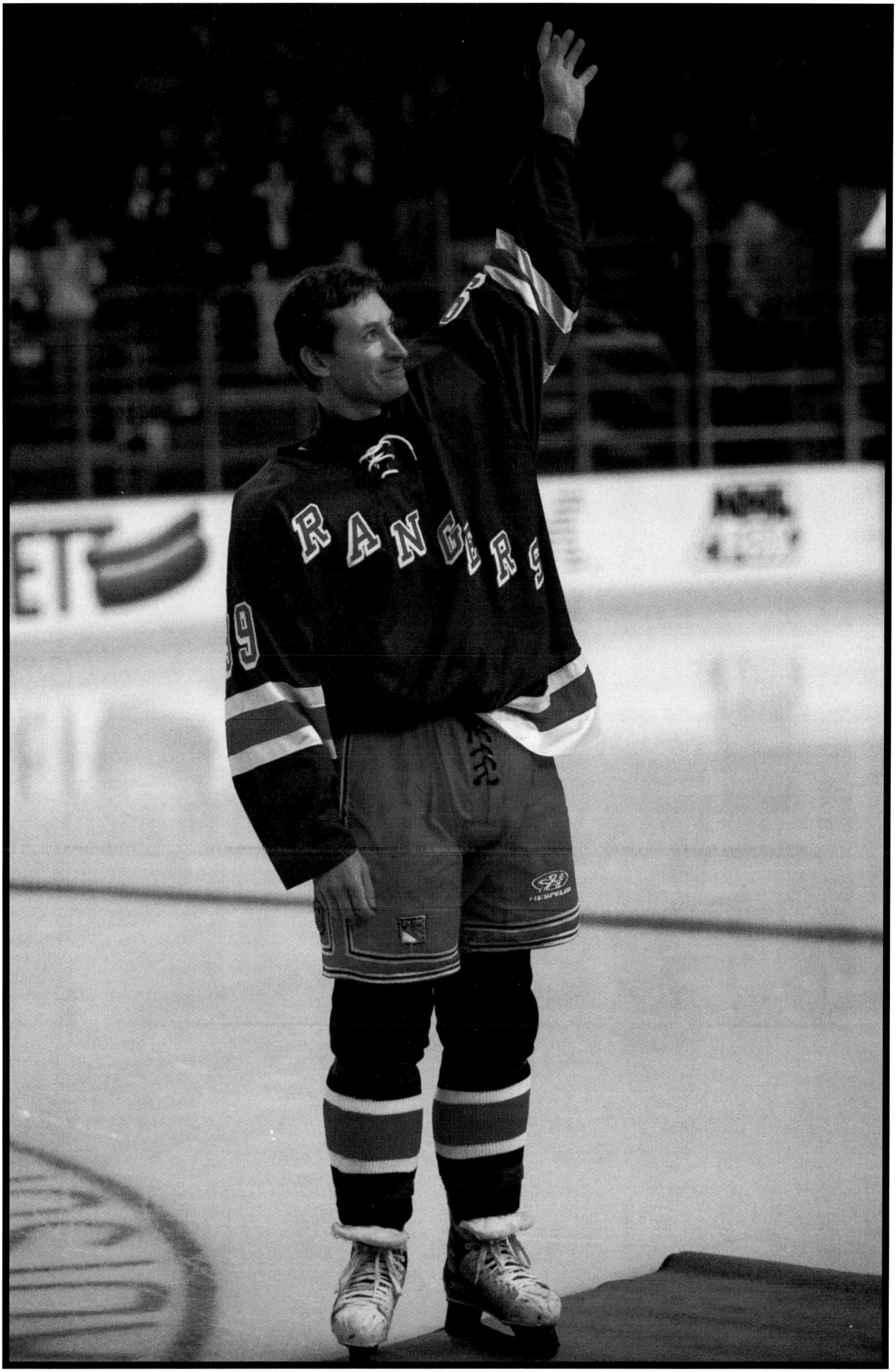

DAILY NEWS

RANGERS NAB THEO WITH EARLY FLEURY

BY JOHN DELLAPINA   JULY 9, 1999

If it truly does take one to know one, then it should come as no surprise that Theo Fleury liked what he saw from Rangers management the moment the free agency period began on July 1.

The quintessential in-your-face, get-it-done-or-out-of-the-way player viewed the Rangers' market-cornering aggressiveness as a major selling point. And upon learning that Garden president Dave Checketts and Rangers president Neil Smith flew to Winnipeg as soon as the market opened, Fleury quickly agreed to become the marquee offensive player on the NHL's biggest market team.

Yesterday afternoon the four-time 40-goal scorer and six-time NHL All-Star formally signed the deal to which he and the Rangers had agreed in principle a week before, a four-year, $28 million contract complete with a limited no-trade clause and a club option on the fourth year.

The money, though lower than most estimates of what Fleury would have commanded on the open market, neverthe-less is eye-popping for a self-proclaimed, small-town Saskatchewan boy who had never before made more than the $2.8 million he earned last season. But it was clear from listening to Fleury during yesterday's conference call that it was the Rangers' full-bore approach that really turned his head.

"It was a situation where, on July 1, we wanted to look at all of our options," Fleury said. "But when Neil and Mr. Checketts came to Winnipeg unexpectedly—there were rumors of that happening, but it wasn't a sure thing to our knowledge—it's nice to be wanted."

The Rangers, who made it clear they were going to open their vault, then blew everybody else out of the water. "The Rangers kind of stated the case that they wanted me and I don't think anybody really wanted to get into a bidding war with them," the diminutive dynamo said. "In the end, the Rangers were very aggressive and they were the team we chose."

OPPOSITE: THE FREE-AGENT SIGNING OF THEO FLEURY WAS THE RANGERS' TOP OFF-SEASON PRIORITY AS THE FRANCHISE LOOKS FORWARD TO THE NEXT CENTURY OF GREAT MEMORIES.

WINNING TRADITIONS...

*the
New York
Rangers
and the
United States
Postal Service*

WHAT IF NEW YORK HAD A BRIDGE
THAT WENT ALL AROUND THE WORLD?

New York is home to hundreds of bridges. Including one that can take you just about

anywhere. It's the bridge called American Airlines®. And over 220* times every business day it

stretches from the New York area to Los Angeles, Chicago, London and hundreds of other

cities around the world. Call your Travel Agent or American at 1-800-433-7300. Or book online

at **www.aa.com** today. Getting where you want

to go is easy. As long as you take the right bridge.

AmericanAirlines
New York's Bridge To The World℠

 member of oneworld

Tom Seaver
Hall of Fame Pitcher and
Chase Middle Market
Spokesperson

No matter how good you are... you need to know the team is behind you.

IN BASEBALL, BUSINESS AND BANKING, IT TAKES A TEAM TO REACH THE TOP.

More growing companies rely on Chase, the leading bank for business

Your Chase Relationship Manager heads a team of professionals dedicated exclusively to growing companies

As your guide and advocate, your Relationship Manager gives you access to credit, cash management, investments, leasing, merger and acquisition advice and financing, derivatives, international – a full range of products and services

We're the leading bank for business because, like you, we play hard. We play to win. And we love the game. Get the best team in banking for your business.

 CHASE

THE RIGHT RELATIONSHIP IS EVERYTHING.®

www.chase.com

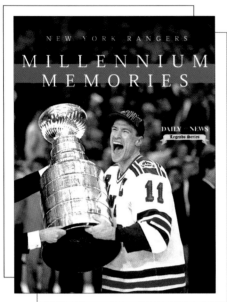